christ

the life of christ - the basis of faith

Student Life Publishing, Inc.

Birmingham, AL

ISBN 0-9755697-1-6

Library of Congress Control Number: 2004108533

Student Life Publishing, Inc.
P.O. Box 36040
Birmingham, AL 35236

To order additional copies of this resource, call the publisher at 888.811.2072
or order online at www.studentlifebiblestudy.com.

Inside royalty-free images provided by MediaBakery (www.mediabakery.com)
Inside illustrations © Rebecca Ruegger (www.ruegger.net)
First Century Jerusalem and Jesus' Journey map illustrations © Bill Latta (www.members.home.net/las)
All other map illustrations by David W. Folds

How to Use This Book

Welcome to an incredible study of the life and teachings of Jesus Christ. You will never study anything that could affect your life more powerfully. This book has been designed to be a companion study to Student Life Bible Study curriculum, year one. You can use this book in several different ways. For example:

1. Study a session each week to deepen your understanding of your small-group Bible study at church.
2. Study this book to keep up with Bible study sessions you miss at church.
3. Meet with a mentor each week to study the sessions together.
4. Study this book on your own to gain a better understanding of the life of Jesus.
5. Use this book as a reference book. Locate events from Jesus' life you want to know more about in the Table of Contents and study those sessions.

You will get the most out of your study if you will follow a few simple suggestions:

1. **Pray** before you begin. God will reveal His truth to you as you seek Him.
2. Keep the **Bible** open. We will prompt you to read certain passages as you study. Even if the passage is familiar, read it carefully.
3. **Write** your responses in this book.
4. Keep a **journal** to record thoughts, questions, commitments, and prayers.

We have included a few things we think will help you as you study:

1. **Special Feature articles** are designed to help you dig a little deeper into some aspect of your study. These articles may answer some of your questions.
2. **Icons** that look like this: ⊤ will occur throughout the study. The Bible teaches **eight truths** we believe are essential to understanding your Christianity. These truths are often referred to as "doctrines." These icons will remind you of the doctrines they represent. Make sure you understand what each icon means. Stop and look them up on page 9 until you are familiar with them.
3. Each session ends with a section called "**Beyond the Basics.**" It includes ideas to expand your study into action. Do at least one in each session. You will probably find this part of the study to be the most rewarding. The first suggestion will always be a **memory verse** to challenge you to hide God's Word in your heart.
4. In each session you will discover we have placed several **sidebars**. These will give you additional word studies or insight into the biblical culture.

God bless you as you study the life of Christ. We pray that the risen Christ will make Himself very clear to you as you draw closer and closer to Him.

Table of Contents

Special Features

Maps and Timelines

Writers

Carol Bailey

Carol is a freelance writer from Alpharetta, GA. She received her music education degree from Troy State University and her Master of Music degree from Southwestern Baptist Theological Seminary. Carol and her husband John have two teenage daughters, Christa and Cara.

Pamela Culbertson

Pamela is the Minister of Youth at Gaston Oaks Baptist Church in Dallas, TX. She earned both an undergraduate and graduate degree from Hardin Simmons University. She is also a graduate of Southwestern Baptist Theological Seminary.

Jimmie L. Davis

Jimmie is Director of Girls' Ministries at First Baptist Church , Spartanburg, SC. She is married to Sam Davis. She is the mother of two adult children and has one granddaughter. She has an Advanced Certificate in Women's Ministry from the New Orleans Baptist Theological Seminary. She is the author of *Virtual You! Love, Beauty, Relationships, Purity, Truth.*

Jim Gantenbein

Jim and his wife Cathy live in Seattle, WA, with their three children Aaron, Alison, and David. Jim has been the Pastor of Youth and Music at Trinity Baptist Church of Lakewood, WA since September 1981. He is a graduate of Oklahoma Baptist University and Southwestern Baptist Theological Seminary.

Jerry Hendrix

Jerry is founder of Horizon Resources, a youth ministry resource company. He also serves as Lead Pastor of Crosspoint Fellowship Church in Abilene, TX. He is married to Sharon, and together they have two teenagers, James and Sarah.

Michael Kelley

Michael lives in Birmingham, AL, with his wife Jana. They welcomed their first child in August 2004. Michael graduated from West Texas A&M University and Beeson Divinity School. Michael is a Camp Director for Student Life.

Scott Kindig

Scott is a 17-year youth ministry veteran. He serves as Youth Ministry Consultant for the Georgia Baptist Convention. Prior to accepting his current position, Scott served on staff for twelve years at Brookwood Baptist Church in Lawrenceville, GA. He and his wife Kim have four children, Seth, Nate, Drew, and Mary Beth. Scott is a graduate of Mercer University and New Orleans Baptist Theological Seminary.

Rhoda Royce

Rhoda is a freelance writer and adjunct instructor at Mississippi College. She and her husband Lee have one son, Mark. Rhoda is a graduate of Belmont University and the University of South Carolina. She has also studied at Vanderbilt University, Ouachita Baptist University, Clemson University, and California State University, Hayward.

Dave Paxton

Dave is the Minister to Students at Olive Baptist Church in Pensacola, FL, where he has served for thirteen years. In his twenty-nine years of student ministry, he has served churches in Tennessee, Texas, and Florida. Dave is a graduate of Southwestern Baptist Theological Seminary. His wife of thirty-two years is Sharon.

Andrew Rupard

Andrew is currently the Youth Minister at Hazelwood Baptist Church in Louisville, KY. He has been married to Beth since 2001; they have no children yet, but do have a dog named Max. Andrew graduated from the University of Kentucky and The Southern Baptist Theological Seminary.

Jay Sedwick, Ph.D.

Jay is an Assistant Professor of Christian Education at Dallas Theological Seminary. He and his wife Laurie have four children, Ana, Lea, Jay, and Kay Lee. Jay received degrees from Pennsylvania State University, Dallas Theological Seminary, and Southwestern Baptist Theological Seminary.

Margaret F. (Margie) Williamson, Ph.D.

Margie is Assistant Professor of Christian Education and the Associate Director of the Extension Center system for the New Orleans Baptist Theological Seminary. She and her husband have two children. Their son Scott is married to Wendy and they have one son, Nate. Their daughter Jenna is a college student.

Cover Design by
Details Design
Birmingham, AL

Editorial Team
Andy Blanks
Birmingham, AL

Jonathan Helms
Birmingham, AL

Paul Kelly
Birmingham, AL

Emily Porter
Birmingham, AL

Chris Preston
Birmingham, AL

Ben Stroup
Nashville, TN

Dwayne Ulmer
Birmingham, AL

Byron Weathersbee
Waco, TX

Graphic Design Team
Liz Gibson
Nashville, TN

David W. Folds
Dawsonville, GA

Key Faith Statements

God Is—There is one and only one true and living God. God is Love. He is an infinite, all-knowing Spirit, perfect in all His attributes, one in essence, eternally existing in three Persons—the Father, Son, and Holy Spirit—each equally deserving of man's worship and obedience.

The Bible Is God's Word—The Bible is God's written revelation to people, divinely given through human authors who were inspired by the Holy Spirit. Therefore, it is truth without any mixture of error. God is the Bible's author. The goal of His Word is the restoration of mankind into His image. We affirm that the Bible is totally sufficient and completely authoritative for matters of life and faith.

People Are God's Treasure—People are God's special treasure, fashioned by Him in His own image as the crowning work of His creation. Everyone has willfully disobeyed God—an act also known as sin—thus inheriting both physical and spiritual death and is in need of salvation. All human beings are born with a sin-nature and into an environment inclined toward sin. As soon as individuals are capable of moral action, they become responsible for their sinful condition. Only by the grace of God through Jesus Christ can they experience salvation.

Jesus Is God and Savior—We believe in the deity of our Lord Jesus Christ, in His virgin birth, and in His sinless life. As God's Son on earth, He was both fully God and fully human. We also believe in His miracles and His substitutionary and atoning death on the cross. Christ rose from the dead, ascended to the right hand of the Father and will return in power and glory.

The Holy Spirit Is God, the Presence and Power—The Holy Spirit is supernatural and sovereign, baptizing all believers into the Body of Christ. He lives within every Christian beginning at the moment of salvation, and then empowers them for effective service as they yield to Him. The Holy Spirit convicts individuals of sin, uses God's Word to mature believers into Christ-likeness and secures them until Christ returns.

Salvation Is By Faith Alone—People were created in the image of God and willfully disobeyed Him, bringing physical and spiritual death. This disobedience is known as sin. All human beings are born with a sin nature, separated from God, and in need of a Savior. That salvation comes only through a faith relationship with Jesus Christ, the Savior, as a person repents of sin and receives Christ's forgiveness and the promise of eternal life. Salvation is instantaneous and accomplished solely by the power of the Holy Spirit through the Word of God. This salvation is wholly of God by grace on the basis of the redeeming work of Jesus Christ, the merit of His shed blood, and not on the basis of human merit or works. All the redeemed are secure in Christ forever.

The Church Is God's Plan—All people who put their faith in Jesus Christ are immediately placed by the Holy Spirit into one united spiritual body, the Church, of which Christ is the head. The primary physical expression of the Church on earth is in autonomous local congregations of baptized believers, associated by covenant in the faith and fellowship of the gospel. The purpose of the Church is to glorify God by taking the Gospel to the entire world and by building its members up in Christ-likeness through the instruction of God's Word, fellowship, service, worship, and prayer.

God Holds the Future—God will bring the world to its appropriate end in His own time and in His own way. At that time, Jesus Christ will return personally and visibly in glory to the earth. Both the saved and unsaved will be resurrected physically to be judged by Christ in righteousness. Those who have received Christ will, in their resurrected and glorified bodies, receive their reward and dwell forever in Heaven with the Lord. Those who have refused Christ will spend eternity in Hell, the place of everlasting punishment. The certain return of Christ is the hope that motivates believers to be faithful in their daily lives.

Introduction

In the history of humanity no other person has been the subject of so much discussion, literature, art, music, and even conflict. He never wrote a book, led an army, or held a public office. He wasn't a gifted athlete or chart-topping musician, nor did He appear on television or in film. Though His name was known by many while He lived on this earth, still many who heard of Him wondered, "Who is this man?" Likewise, for two thousand years since that time humanity has wrestled with the question of His identity. Often just the mention of His name confronts people with the necessity of choosing how they would respond to Him.

For centuries before His birth, people anticipated His arrival and longed for the impact He would make. In the centuries since, countless people have responded to His love and have been transformed by the Spirit He left behind. He is the One who split time with His coming and for whose return all creation awaits. He is Jesus Christ, the Son of God.

Through the sessions in this study on the life of Christ, you will encounter history's central figure. Beginning with Old Testament prophecy about His coming and going all the way through Jesus' own prophetic pronouncements about His return, these lessons will give you an in-depth look at Jesus Christ in a way you may never have seen before. While these sessions will provide you with an understanding of the general order of the events in Jesus' life, sometimes they will be grouped by theme rather than according to chronological order. Themes will focus on Jesus and His disciples, the miracles Jesus performed, the parables Jesus told, and other people Jesus encountered. You will also study Jesus' birth and His early life, the beginnings of His ministry, and His actions and teachings at the end of His earthly life, including His death, resurrection, and ascension.

Through this study, you will discover why Jesus came to earth. As you witness His miracles, listen to His teachings, and contemplate His lifestyle during the three-year period of His public ministry, you will also be confronted with the question, *Who is this man?*

While these lessons are designed to lead you in discovering more about the life and work of Jesus Christ, they are much more than just a series of history lessons. Each one points to the potential impact Jesus Christ can have in every person's life today. Above all, this study series has been developed to help you discover the peace, joy, hope, love, strength, and life that are offered to you as a result of what Jesus did so long ago and continues to do today.

The journey to a fuller knowledge of Christ begins here. Are you ready?

-Greg Miller, General Editor, Bible Commentary

New Testament Timeline

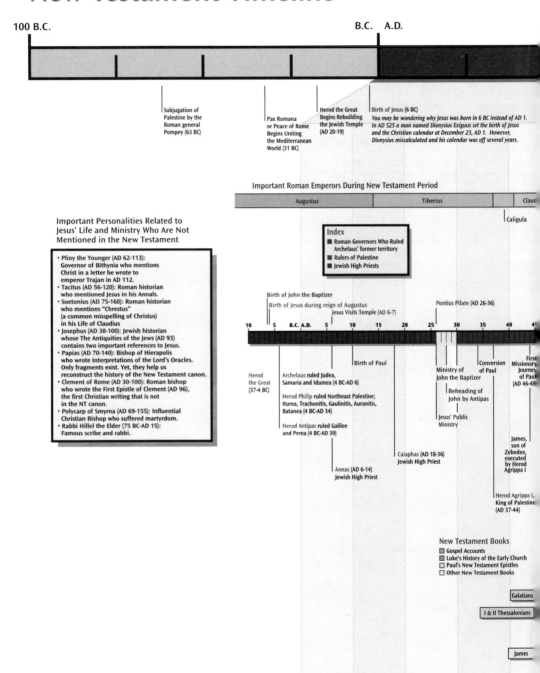

100 B.C.   B.C.   A.D.

Subjugation of Palestine by the Roman general Pompey (63 BC)

Pax Romana or Peace of Rome Begins Uniting the Mediterranean World (31 BC)

Herod the Great Begins Rebuilding the Jewish Temple (AD 20-19)

Birth of Jesus (6 BC)
You may be wondering why Jesus was born in 6 BC instead of AD 1. In AD 525 a man named Dionysius Exiguus set the birth of Jesus and the Christian calendar at December 23, AD 1. However, Dionysius miscalculated and his calendar was off several years.

Important Roman Emperors During New Testament Period

Augustus	Tiberius	Claud

Caligula

Important Personalities Related to Jesus' Life and Ministry Who Are Not Mentioned in the New Testament

- Pliny the Younger (AD 62-113): Governor of Bithynia who mentions Christ in a letter he wrote to emperor Trajan in AD 112.
- Tacitus (AD 56-120): Roman historian who mentioned Jesus in his Annals.
- Suetonius (AD 75-160): Roman historian who mentions "Chrestus" (a common misspelling of Christus) in his Life of Claudius
- Josephus (AD 38-100): Jewish historian whose The Antiquities of the Jews (AD 93) contains two important references to Jesus.
- Papias (AD 70-140): Bishop of Hierapolis who wrote Interpretations of the Lord's Oracles. Only fragments exist. Yet, they help us reconstruct the history of the New Testament canon.
- Clement of Rome (AD 30-100): Roman bishop who wrote the First Epistle of Clement (AD 96), the first Christian writing that is not in the NT canon.
- Polycarp of Smyrna (AD 69-155): Influential Christian Bishop who suffered martyrdom.
- Rabbi Hillel the Elder (75 BC-AD 15): Famous scribe and rabbi.

Index
- ■ Roman Governors Who Ruled Archelaus' former territory
- ■ Rulers of Palestine
- ■ Jewish High Priests

Birth of John the Baptizer
Birth of Jesus during reign of Augustus
Jesus Visits Temple (AD 6-7)

Pontius Pilate (AD 26-36)

10   5   B.C. A.D.   5   10   15   20   25   30   35   40   4

Herod the Great (37-4 BC)

Archelaus ruled Judea, Samaria and Idumea (4 BC-AD 6)

Herod Philip ruled Northeast Palestine; Iturea, Trachonitis, Gaulinitis, Auranitis, Batanea (4 BC-AD 34)

Herod Antipas ruled Galilee and Perea (4 BC-AD 39)

Birth of Paul

Ministry of John the Baptizer

Conversion of Paul

First Missionary Journey of Paul (AD 46-48)

Beheading of John by Antipas

Jesus' Public Ministry

James, son of Zebedee, executed by Herod Agrippa I

Caiaphas (AD 18-36) Jewish High Priest

Annas (AD 6-14) Jewish High Priest

Herod Agrippa I, King of Palestine (AD 37-44)

New Testament Books
- ▨ Gospel Accounts
- ■ Luke's History of the Early Church
- ▢ Paul's New Testament Epistles
- ▢ Other New Testament Books

Galatians

I & II Thessalonians

James

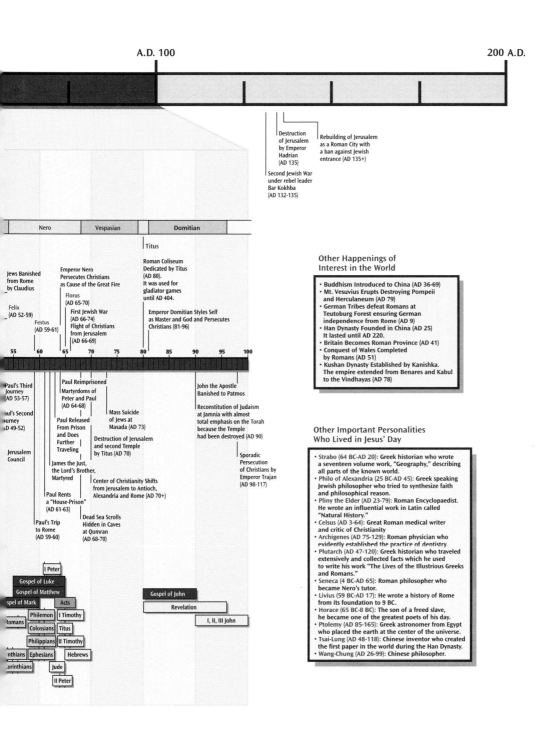

A.D. 100   **200 A.D.**

Destruction of Jerusalem by Emperor Hadrian (AD 135)

Rebuilding of Jerusalem as a Roman City with a ban against Jewish entrance (AD 135+)

Second Jewish War under rebel leader Bar Kokhba (AD 132-135)

Nero	Vespasian	Domitian

Titus

Jews Banished from Rome by Claudius

Emperor Nero Persecutes Christians as Cause of the Great Fire

Roman Coliseum Dedicated by Titus (AD 80). It was used for gladiator games until AD 404.

Florus (AD 65-70)

Felix (AD 52-59)

First Jewish War (AD 66-74)
Flight of Christians from Jerusalem (AD 66-69)

Festus (AD 59-61)

Emperor Domitian Styles Self as Master and God and Persecutes Christians (81-96)

55   60   65   70   75   80   85   90   95   100

Paul's Third Journey (AD 53-57)

Paul Reimprisoned
Martyrdoms of Peter and Paul (AD 64-68)

John the Apostle Banished to Patmos

Paul's Second Journey (AD 49-52)

Paul Released From Prison and Does Further Traveling

Mass Suicide of Jews at Masada (AD 73)

Reconstitution of Judaism at Jamnia with almost total emphasis on the Torah because the Temple had been destroyed (AD 90)

Jerusalem Council

James the Just, the Lord's Brother, Martyred

Destruction of Jerusalem and second Temple by Titus (AD 70)

Center of Christianity Shifts from Jerusalem to Antioch, Alexandria and Rome (AD 70+)

Sporadic Persecution of Christians by Emperor Trajan (AD 98-117)

Paul Rents a "House-Prison" (AD 61-63)

Dead Sea Scrolls Hidden in Caves at Qumran (AD 68-70)

Paul's Trip to Rome (AD 59-60)

I Peter
Gospel of Luke
Gospel of Matthew
Gospel of Mark   Acts
Philemon   I Timothy
Romans   Colossians   Titus
Philippians   II Timothy
...nthians   Ephesians   Hebrews
...orinthians   Jude
II Peter

Gospel of John
Revelation
I, II, III John

Other Happenings of Interest in the World

- Buddhism Introduced to China (AD 36-69)
- Mt. Vesuvius Erupts Destroying Pompeii and Herculaneum (AD 79)
- German Tribes defeat Romans at Teutoburg Forest ensuring German independence from Rome (AD 9)
- Han Dynasty Founded in China (AD 25) It lasted until AD 220.
- Britain Becomes Roman Province (AD 41)
- Conquest of Wales Completed by Romans (AD 51)
- Kushan Dynasty Established by Kanishka. The empire extended from Benares and Kabul to the Vindhayas (AD 78)

Other Important Personalities Who Lived in Jesus' Day

- Strabo (64 BC-AD 20): Greek historian who wrote a seventeen volume work, "Geography," describing all parts of the known world.
- Philo of Alexandria (25 BC-AD 45): Greek speaking Jewish philosopher who tried to synthesize faith and philosophical reason.
- Pliny the Elder (AD 23-79): Roman Encyclopaedist. He wrote an influential work in Latin called "Natural History."
- Celsus (AD 3-64): Great Roman medical writer and critic of Christianity
- Archigenes (AD 75-129): Roman physician who evidently established the practice of dentistry.
- Plutarch (AD 47-120): Greek historian who traveled extensively and collected facts which he used to write his work "The Lives of the Illustrious Greeks and Romans."
- Seneca (4 BC-AD 65): Roman philosopher who became Nero's tutor.
- Livius (59 BC-AD 17): He wrote a history of Rome from its foundation to 9 BC.
- Horace (65 BC-8 BC): The son of a freed slave, he became one of the greatest poets of his day.
- Ptolemy (AD 85-165): Greek astronomer from Egypt who placed the earth at the center of the universe.
- Tsai-Lung (AD 48-118): Chinese inventor who created the first paper in the world during the Han Dynasty.
- Wang-Chung (AD 26-99): Chinese philosopher.

Jesus' Trip to Jerusalem

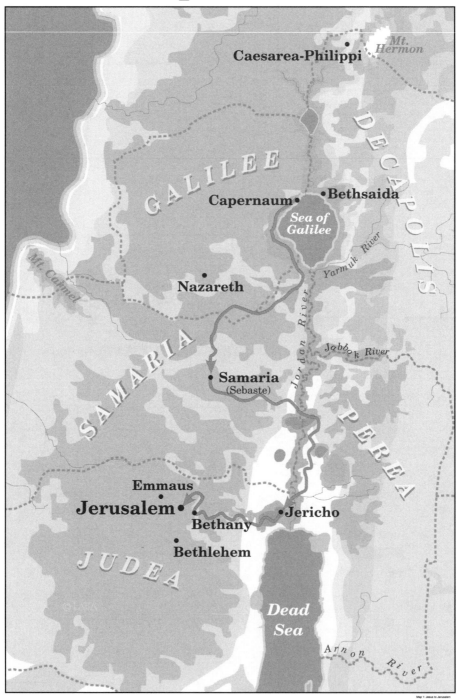

How to Handle the Truth

by Brian Manuel

Have you ever been accused of not being able to handle the truth? You know what I mean. Someone slams you. When you respond negatively, they say, "I'm just telling you the truth. You just can't handle the truth." Regardless of whether or not it is true, it is a pretty serious accusation. All of us would like to think that when confronted with the truth, we are mature enough to handle it. What about when the "Truth" is God's Word? Can you handle Scripture? Are you able to study the Bible and gain from the experience?

I remember a time when a youth worker at my church asked me if I was faithfully studying my Bible. It really threw me for a loop! My youth pastor always encouraged me to read my Bible every day. He said it was essential for a healthy relationship with Christ. But *study* the Bible? Why? Were we having a pop quiz on Sunday? I knew the basics, but I hadn't really *studied* the Bible, at least not on my own. I began to squirm in my seat.

The truth was I didn't have a clue what it meant to study my Bible, and to be honest the term "study" scared me a little. I had visions of sitting at my desk at home slaving over my biology textbook, trying to decipher the sloppy notes I had written in class, hoping for a good grade on the next test. Studying the Bible is a bit different. Grades matter when studying for things like English and math, but when it comes to knowing God's Word, it's more of a "pass or fail issue;" the only way you can fail is simply not to do it.

Have you ever been in a worship service or a retreat and had one of those "Ah-ha!" moments? "Ah-ha!" moments are those times when the truth of God's Word is revealed in wonderful ways, and for a moment, everything makes sense. I'll let you in on a little secret. Most of the best "Ah-ha!" moments–the very best life-changing information you hear from parents, teachers, and youth leaders–are located in the Bible. A strong relationship with God starts with a strong relationship with His Word.

Do you know what the Bible says about studying Scripture? Second Timothy 3:16-17 says, "All scripture is inspired by God and is useful to teach us what is true and to make us realize what is wrong in our lives. It straightens us out and teaches us to do what is right. It is God's way of preparing us in every way, fully equipped for every good thing God wants us to do." (NLT) Psalms 119:9 puts it even simpler. "How can a young person stay pure? By obeying your word" (NLT). But how do you do Bible study?

Tips for Handling the Truth

To do effective Bible study, take your time. Don't try to study too much Scripture in one sitting. Find a comfortable and quite place. Turn off the TV or stereo so you won't be distracted.

Pray before you get started. Ask God to help you understand what you are about to study and how you might apply it to your life. Read a section or two then stop and reflect on what you have read. Get a journal to take down specific thoughts the Holy Spirit brings to your mind.

Book Study

A good idea for beginners is the Bible-book study approach. Study one book at a time in its entirety. The great evangelist Billy Graham encouraged those who were just starting to study the Bible to begin with the book of John, a book all about Christ and His love for humankind.

The use of a good Bible commentary may help you. Commentaries are books of educated and researched comments about each Scripture verse. In most commentaries, each verse is analyzed and broken down into easy-to-understand sentences. A commentary can help you closely examine verses as you read them. Begin a file on paper or your computer of the notes and insights you get from each book, verse by verse.

Character Study

A character study examines the life of a particular person in the Bible. Select a biblical character, such as King David. Use a Bible dictionary to read about the person. Then, use a biblical concordance to locate passages in the Bible that mention this person. (A concordance is a Bible study tool that will identify every place in Scripture where a particular word is used.) A character study can help you learn how God worked through an individual to accomplish His will. As you study, ask yourself what this person's life has to say to you about how you should live.

Topical Study

Discovering what the Bible has to say about a particular topic (such as love, prayer, or marriage) is another approach to handling the Truth. Use a Bible concordance or index to locate every passage on the topic you have selected. (A topical Bible is also another valuable tool for this type of Bible study.) Read each passage you find and take notes on the truths you discover. Summarize key thoughts you come across in your study. Be sure to jot down what you are learning about how to walk with Christ.

Don't get discouraged if you fail to study your Bible for a while. The key to success is to pick it back up as quickly as you can and keep after it. Set some goals for yourself on the types and number of personal Bible studies you would like to complete in a certain period of time. You'll find it becomes a part of your life very quickly. You will also be amazed at how much of what you have been studying comes to mind as you go through life. If you take the time to study God's Word on a regular basis you will find that those "Ah-Ha!" moments don't just happen at summer camp and youth retreats. They can actually happen daily in your room when it's just you, your Bible, and God.

Events in the Life of Jesus: Public Ministry (A.D. 26-30)

A.D. 26	A.D. 27	A.D. 28	A.D. 29	A.D. 30
Jesus' Baptism by John	Jesus' Sermon on the Mount	John the Baptist's Imprisonment	Jesus' Parables on Lost Things	Jesus' Parable of the Unmerciful Servant
Temptations of Jesus	Jesus' Parable of the Sower	John the Baptist's Beheading	Peter's Confession of Jesus as the Christ	Jesus' Parable of the Vineyard Workers
		Jesus' Feeding of the Five Thousand		Jesus Predicts His Death Again
Jesus Chooses His Disciples	Jesus' Parable of the Mustard Seed and Yeast		Jesus Establishes His Church	
Jesus' First Miracle at Cana of Galilee			The Transfiguration	Jesus Raises Lazarus from the Dead
				Jesus Appears to Many Persons over a Forty Day Post-Resurrection Ministry
Nicodemus Meets Jesus			Jesus Predicts His Death	
			Jesus' Teaching on the Greatest in the Kingdom	Jesus Restores Peter
The Samaritan Woman Meets Jesus				Jesus Gives the Great Commission
			Jesus Sends Seventy Disciples out on Mission	
The Centurion's Faith				Jesus Ascends into Heaven
Jesus Calms the Storm			The Parable of the Good Samaritan	The Holy Spirit Comes Upon the Believers in Jerusalem Fifty Days (Pentecost) after Jesus' Crucifixion

Jesus' Passion Week (A.D. 30)

Sunday	Jesus' Triumphal Entry into Jerusalem
Monday	Jesus Cleanses the Temple/Jesus' Parable of the Wedding Banquet
Tuesday	Jesus Admonishes the Pharisee/Mary Anoints Jesus at Bethany
Thursday	Jesus' Last Supper with His Disciples/Jesus Washes the Disciples' Feet
	Jesus' Arrest in the Garden of Gethsemane/Jesus' Trial Before the Sanhedrin
Friday	Jesus' Roman Trial, Crucifixion, and Burial
Sunday	Jesus' Resurrection

How Did They Know **Before** He Came

 Isaiah 9:1-7

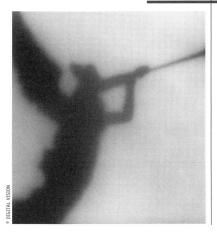

© DIGITAL VISION

MEMORY VERSE

For to us a child is born, to us a son is given, and the government will be on his shoulders. And he will be called Wonderful Counselor, Mighty God, Everlasting Father, Prince of Peace. Isaiah 9:6

"Radio has no future."

"X-rays will prove to be a hoax."

"Heavier-than-air flying machines are impossible."

—*Statements attributed to one of the nineteenth century's most renowned scientists*

"There is no reason anyone would want a computer in their home."

—*Statement attributed to a technology company president in the 1970s*

Who Knew?

Human beings like to speculate about the future. We often think we know what's going to happen. Sometimes we are right, but often we are wrong. It can be funny when we "read" the future wrongly; but sometimes it's not funny at all.

A murder suspect had spent 11 years incarcerated before being released from a Utah prison. Despite his criminal record, he was judged to be a low risk for violence and released. Six months later, he killed a college student. "We're kind of in the dark ages when it comes to making predictions about criminal behavior. We're at about the same level as meteorologists or weathermen. Their forecasts are too often wrong and so are ours," said Jack Levin, director of the Brudnick Center on Violence and Conflict at Northeastern University.[1]

What are some kinds of predictions about the future "experts" often get wrong? (One example is done for you.)

1. Which sports team will win a game

2. _____   5. _____

3. _____   6. _____

4. _____   7. _____

We human beings fail to predict the future accurately because we live in the present. God, on the other hand, lives in eternity. He is above and beyond time, and He makes no mistakes. When He says something will happen, it will happen. 🔔 Around 2,700 years ago, through His prophet Isaiah, He shared some good news with some people in a bad situation.

One-minute History of Redemption

Need a little context for Isaiah 9? Reading the following paragraph should get you ready to understand this Bible study.

In the Garden of Eden, Eve and Adam gave in to temptation. They had to leave the Garden, but God revealed His intent to redeem them. (See Genesis 3:15.) A long time after Noah's flood, God called Abraham to follow Him away from his home; through obedience, Abraham became the father of the Hebrew people. After many years of slavery in Egypt and after wandering in the wilderness, God's people began to conquer Canaan, the land God promised them. Different Hebrew tribes were given different areas to inhabit; eventually, they were united under King Saul and then under a greater king, David. Even later, the Hebrews' kingdom was divided into Israel, the northern kingdom, and Judah, the southern kingdom. Over and over, God's people sinned by ignoring

Prophets—Lots of people claim to speak for God. Some we can trust, some we can't. The prophets who spoke for God in the Bible had several traits in common:

- True prophets always directed people toward the worship of the Lord alone (Deuteronomy 13:1).
- A true prophet doesn't claim to know everything. He knows and speaks the messages God gives Him. These words must be fulfilled (Ezekiel 33:33).
- A true prophet speaks God's revelation whether it is popular or not (Jeremiah 37:1-21).
- A true prophet does not change his message from God to please people or to receive money (Micah 3:5).

His laws and worshiping idols. Through messengers, called **prophets**, God warned the Hebrew people that punishment would come. The Assyrians, a fierce enemy, would invade and finally conquer the northern kingdom; a similar fate awaited the southern kingdom at the hands of the Babylonians. During the years of invasion and destruction, the people's suffering was extreme. Once again, God's prophets spoke words of warning. Yet they also spoke, again and again, of good news: God would use a great king to redeem His people. 🚶🚶

Why Hope for the Future?

Read Isaiah 9:1-5, remembering the unfortunate condition of the people who first received this prophecy.

Record a promise God made through Isaiah in verse 1.

When would it happen?

What blessings would the people of Israel experience?

The Hope for the Future

In the United States, the President is the leader of the entire nation. The American people are dependant on his leadership for the country. Write four characteristics of a leader you would vote for.

Take a look at what you've written. Which characteristic is most important? Which would you give up if you couldn't get all of them in one leader? Cross out any unnecessary traits and circle the ones you can't do without.

Politicians make a lot of promises, especially during an election year. Record some typical election year promises:

Next, check the promises politicians always keep.

Zebulun and Naphtali—In Isaiah 9:1 the lands of Zebulun and Naphtali are mentioned as having been humbled. These two regions were two of the first places to be devastated in the invasion of the Assyrian army. Just like Jesus offers us hope today, the promise of the Messiah served as a great beacon of hope for the people in these war-torn regions.

Read Isaiah 9:6-9. Isaiah prophesied about a **great leader** more than 700 years before Jesus Christ was born. Record four names given to that leader found in these verses. Then draw a line from each name to its meaning. ▼

①   **a great king who carries out a wise and marvelous plan of action**

②   **the all-conquering powerful deity**

③   **the eternal provider and protector**

④   **the ruler whose reign brings well-being to individuals and groups**

The government will be on his shoulders—In the NIV, verse 6 says "the government will be on his shoulders." The Hebrew word *mi´râ*; literally translates as "rule" or "dominion." While many people incorrectly expected that the Messiah would be a political ruler, we know today Jesus' kingship applies to all creation throughout all eternity. When we accept Christ, we enter into a relationship where He becomes the ruler of our lives, and we become the servants in His glorious Kingdom.

BEYOND THE BASICS!

- Memorize Isaiah 9:6.
- Email to a friend God's promise you chose from the Bible.
- Reflect on several Bible promises (e.g., Deut. 4:29; Matt. 5:7, 9; John 3:16; Heb. 13:5). Choose one to memorize.
- Plan a way to act on God's promise. For instance, you might react to being excluded by someone by considering God's promise to include all those who trust Jesus (John 3:16).
- With your family, choose a family promise to memorize and use to encourage each other.

Now record the promises God made through Isaiah about the Messiah in verses 6-9:

As you record the promises, check those that came true in Jesus Christ.

Trust for the Future

Politicians don't always keep their promises. God has been keeping His for all time and eternity. He promised to redeem us through the Savior He would send, and He did.

The people who heard Isaiah's good news had a lot of suffering to go through before the promise was fulfilled. Despite the confusion and problems of their lives, God was always working to accomplish His purposes at the right time.

---

1. *Portland* [Maine] *Press Herald*, November 11, 2003.

02. God's Great Gift

 Luke 2:1-20

MEMORY VERSE

Today in the town of David a Savior has been born to you; he is Christ the Lord.

Luke 2:11

The Best Christmas Gift Ever

Once in a while, a great Christmas gift makes the news. Here are my favorites:

Army Cpl. Christopher MacIntyre, Jr., of Stuart, Florida, served with the U.S. Army's 4th Infantry Division in Iraq. For two weeks at Christmas, he came home to spend time with family and friends. Betty Smith, a family friend, had sent MacIntyre many letters and packages but hadn't met him until he returned. She called his visit home "the best Christmas gift that anyone could have given me. It's the highlight of my year."[1]

Matthew Callison was diagnosed with cardiomyopathy on his twenty-eighth birthday in October 2003. His condition became even more serious, and a heart transplant was required. Just a few days after Christmas, he received a new heart from a man who had died after suffering a brain injury.[2]

Zhong Mi, a Chinese infant eleven days old, was abandoned in Jin Ahou, China. Today she is known as Jaimi. She has been adopted by Americans.

Barb and Mark Stickel traveled to China to bring her home. The Stickels plan to tell Jaimi about her background; her mother says, "The day she asks about it, I'll tell her, 'God told us about you in China and we came to get you.' She is by far our best Christmas gift ever."[3]

What was the greatest Christmas gift you ever received?

Getting a gift you like for Christmas is nice. Getting something totally unexpected can be incredible. But the greatest gift is a person—Jesus! Perhaps you have never thought of Jesus as a gift, but that is what He was. When we were enslaved in sin, God provided the only gift that could redeem us: His Son. ⊤

The Gift of a King
You have heard the Christmas story many times. You know parts of it by heart. It is a story everyone needs to hear, but it can lose its wonder with repetition. Set aside all you know about Christmas. Read Luke 2:1-7 as if you had never heard the words before. Then write a few impressions in the margin of this book.

Redemption—Redemption means deliverance by payment of a price. Jesus Christ has paid the price of all sin for those who accept His salvation.

Mary was probably a young teenager, but something extraordinary happened to her. God had chosen her to be Jesus' mother. It was impossible for her to have a child; she had never been with a man sexually. But, God did the impossible. Shortly before her Child was due, she and Joseph, her fiancé, traveled from Nazareth, their hometown. Their destination was Bethlehem, the birthplace of Israel's greatest king, David. This 85 mile-trip must have been difficult for an expectant mother.

The Gift of Humility
Look at Luke 2:6-7 again. No truly suitable place was found for Jesus' birth. After His birth, He was placed in a feeding trough for animals at a crude lodging place for caravans passing through Bethlehem. He was wrapped tightly in strips of cloth, an ancient practice still followed in some cultures today; this was thought to help limbs grow straight.

The Roman Census—At this time, Rome ruled much of the Mediterranean world. The emperor Caesar Augustus had decreed a census of the empire. Citizens were required to travel to the place of their ancestry. Joseph (and probably Mary) descended from King David.

Why was Jesus born in Bethlehem?— Jesus was born in this specific city because it fulfilled one of many prophecies about the coming Messiah. This prophecy was found in Micah 5:2: "But you, Bethlehem Ephrathah, though you are small among the clans of Judah, out of you will come for me one who will be ruler over Israel, whose origins are from old ancient times."

Shepherds—Sheep were significant in Bible times. They provided food, clothing, milk, and leather, and they were used for sacrifices in the Temple worship. On the other hand, the people who took care of sheep weren't highly respected. They lived a rough, mostly outdoor life and couldn't meet all the ceremonial cleanliness standards of Judaism. Yet one of the ironies of the Christmas story is that shepherds were the first to hear the news of Jesus the Savior's birth.

Had Mary and Joseph arrived into a modern city, they might have been sent to a homeless shelter. Few kings are born in homeless shelters, but that might be a way to think about what happened. What do you think the significance is of God's Son being born in such a setting?

The Gift for All

Read Luke 2:8-12. Can you imagine the total surprise and fear the **shepherds** felt during that experience? There was nothing ordinary about this child being born. Messengers from God are not common, even in the Bible, but they had surrounded His birth. His birth had been promised by prophets hundreds of years before. Jesus would reveal God to humanity like never before. He would offer God's love to us dramatically by laying down His life in payment for our sins. ▼

What are the main difficulties you experience in life? List a few.

What are the main difficulties all human beings experience in life? List a few more.

Look back at the Christmas gifts described at the beginning of this session. Each gift brought great joy because it helped solve a problem. What if One Gift could make all human struggles worthwhile? What if One Gift could bring everyone hope of eternal life?

Just thinking about the gift of Christ makes Christians feel like singing. That is just what happened when the gift was announced. A "great company of the heavenly host" appeared praising God for His greatest gift.

You may not feel important, but God cares about you and loves you. Just as He announced His gift to simple shepherds, He wants you to know that He loves you too. ⍦

The Gift to Share!

After the amazing announcement, the shepherds ran to Bethlehem to find the "sign" the angel had told them: the baby lying in a manger.

The Gift Flow Chart

Heard the News.

Went to...

Found...

and...

Spread...

and...

Read Luke 2:15-20. Complete the chart at the left with the shepherds' actions.

Some people hear the news of God's great gift of salvation, accept that news of salvation, receive God's forgiveness, and then stop. Too often, they don't share the gift with everyone else.

What makes you hesitant to share the news of God's greatest gift?

Write the name of a friend or relative: _____

Write a way you could share God's gift with that person.

BEYOND THE BASICS!

- Memorize Luke 2:11.
- Read Matthew 1 for more information about Jesus' birth.
- Find a Christmas carol book or a favorite Christmas CD. Sing or listen to one joyful praise of Jesus' birth each day this week.
- When a friend shares a problem this week, listen with respect and concern. Also share how God's greatest gift can bring joy and redemption into your friend's life and situation.

1. Tyko, Kelly. "This Gift Was Wrapped in Fatigues." 20 Dec. 2003: *The Stuart News* (FL): A1.
2. "Heart Transplant the Best Christmas Gift Ever," Copyright 2003, The Evangelical Covenant Church <http://www.covchurch.org/cov/news/item3440.html>
3. Bailey, Laurie. "From Across the World, The Best Christmas Gift." 24 Dec. 2003: *Pittsburgh Post-Gazette* (Pennsylvania): EZ1. Copyright 2003 P.G. Publishing Co.

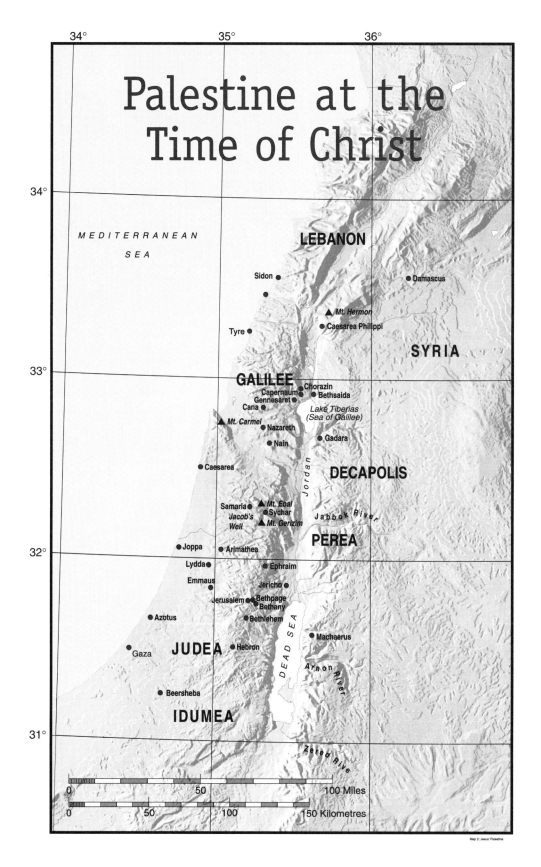

Palestine at the
Time of Christ

34°   35°   36°

34°

MEDITERRANEAN

SEA

LEBANON

Sidon ●

● Damascus

▲ *Mt. Hermon*

Tyre ●

● Caesarea Philppi

SYRIA

33°

GALILEE

Chorazin ●

Capernaum ● ● Bethsaida

Gennesaret ●

Cana ●   *Lake Tiberias*
(Sea of Galilee)

▲ *Mt. Carmel*   ● Nazareth

● Nain   ● Gadara

● Caesarea

DECAPOLIS

Jordan

Samaria ● ▲ *Mt. Ebal*

Jacob's   ● Sychar

Well   ▲ *Mt. Gerizim*

Jabbok River

PEREA

32°

● Joppa   ● Arimathea

Lydda ●   ● Ephraim

Emmaus ●   Jericho ●

Jerusalem ● ● Bethpage
   ● Bethany

● Azotus   ● Bethlehem

DEAD SEA

● Machaerus

Gaza ●   **JUDEA**   ● Hebron

Arnon River

● Beersheba

IDUMEA

31°

Zered River

0   50   100 Miles

0   50   100   150 Kilometres

Map 2: Jesus' Palestine

© DIGITAL VISION

MEMORY VERSE

Those who accepted his message were baptized, and about three thousand were added to their number that day.

Acts 2:41

Rolling Snowballs

Eldrick was hardly even out of the crib when his father began toting him to golf courses and driving ranges. Little Eldrick would mimic his father's swing as he watched him hit the ball. At age two, Eldrick putted with actor Bob Hope on a TV talk show. At age three, he shot a 48 on nine holes. Two years later he was featured in *Golf Digest*.

Like a snowball rolling down a hill, Eldrick gained momentum in his golf game. He won the Optimist International Junior tournament six times before his 16th birthday and played in his first professional tournament at age 16. Eldrick has become one of the most famous golfers of our time, though he is better known by the nickname his father gave him: "Tiger" Woods.

A little snowball starts rolling down a hill. It gets bigger as it consumes everything in its path. Some things take off like that. Tiger's golf career seemed to gain momentum from the first time he picked up a club. What have you seen begin small and grow quickly? Has that ever happened in your life?

Jesus' Ministry Begins

We have very little information about the first 30 years of Jesus' life. Then, He went to His cousin John to be **baptized**. All of a sudden things started to happen. His ministry seemed to gain momentum from that point until His death.

Read Matthew 3:13-17. Why do you think John objected when Jesus went to him to be baptized?

What do you think John meant when he told Jesus, "I need to be baptized by you"?

Despite John's protests, he did baptize Jesus. John must have been aware of his own sinfulness when he drew Jesus into the water. Two miraculous things happened right after the baptism. Write them here:

V. 16–The _____

descended onto Jesus as a

_____.

V. 17–A voice from heaven said,

"This is my _____ whom I

love; with him I am _____

_____.

Baptized—The Greek word the Bible uses for baptize is *baptizo*. It means "to dip in water" or "immerse." John the Baptist called people to repent of sins and be baptized. This baptism was a ceremonial cleansing of sin. The reason Jesus, who was without sin, should be baptized has been discussed by Bible students for thousands of years. Most agree Jesus wanted to identify with sinful humanity and give us an example to follow. Later, Jesus instructed His disciples to "go and make disciples, baptizing them in the name of the Father and of the Son and of the Holy Spirit" (Matt. 28:19). ▼

All three persons of the Trinity are involved in the picture of Jesus' baptism. The Spirit descended as a dove. The Father spoke from heaven. Jesus' mission to the world was affirmed by God—Father, Son and Holy Spirit. **GOD**

The Testimony of John

Read John 1:29-34. As a result of Jesus' baptism, John recognized who Jesus was—and whose He was—and told others about Him. Answer the following questions.

1. Who did John the Baptist tell others Jesus was? (v. 29)

2. How did John know Jesus was the Messiah? (v. 33)

3. What was John's conclusion about Jesus' identity? (v. 34)

Follow the path of the snowball.
Jesus' obedience in baptism revealed His identity to John the Baptist.
John the Baptist told others who Jesus was.
Some who heard about Jesus passed it along to others.
Many people came to know Christ as a result of hearing about Jesus (Acts 2:41).
People who hear about Jesus today are still coming to know Christ.
Every time someone comes to Christ the snowball picks up steam.
Every time a new believer is baptized, they tell the story of Jesus all over again and the snowball picks up more steam.

Baby Steps

Bill Murray played a lovable neurotic in the movie *What About Bob?* Bob was afraid of everything: afraid of riding in elevators, afraid of germs, afraid of public transportation, afraid of ... well, you get the picture. Bob had so many phobias he could not function in society. Finally, he went for help from a self-important pop psychologist named Leo Melvin. Dr. Melvin had no time for Bob. He shoved a copy of his recently published book, *Baby Steps,* into Bob's hands. He told Bob he could get over his fears by breaking them into small achievable successes. For example, he could conquer his fear of getting on the elevator by succeeding in walking out of the office, then walking down the hall, then pushing the button, then stepping on the elevator. And, Dr. Melvin pushed Bob out of his office. The amazing thing is Bob was able to use Dr. Melvin's instruction to overcome some of his fear.

This movie has an important lesson about your walk with Christ. Your life can be hugely successful for the Kingdom of God. But you will need to take it step by step.

The Lamb of God—As long as the temple stood, a priest offered a lamb as a sacrifice for the sins of the people every morning and every evening of every day. When John called Jesus the "Lamb of God," he may not have understood the implications of what he was saying. However, Jesus was to be the complete sacrifice for the sins of those who would place their trust in Him. In fact, the prophets had said that the Messiah would be "like a gentle lamb led to the slaughter." (See Jeremiah 11:19; also Isaiah 53:7.) ▼

D. L. Moody said that if baptism saved people, he would put a tub in a pick-up truck and drive down the street dunking everyone in sight. Only a relationship with Jesus can save a person.

The first step God has challenged you to take once you have a relationship with Jesus Christ is baptism. If you have been baptized, think about that experience. Describe your baptism here:

 BEYOND THE BASICS!

- Memorize Acts 2:41.
- Rent "What About Bob" and watch it with a friend who has accepted Jesus, but has yet to be baptized. After the movie, talk with that friend about taking that first step of obedience to Christ in baptism.
- Request to be trained as a decision counselor by your youth pastor, youth leader, or pastor. Let them know you want to continue the ripple effect Jesus started in His own baptism.
- Search *Go Magazine*'s website (www.go.studentz.com) for an article on baptism. Make sure you have a good understanding of what the Bible teaches about baptism.

Does Baptism Save You?

Ephesians 2:8-10 reminds us salvation is by grace and through faith. Salvation is not achieved by doing good things—not even baptism. Baptism is a step of our life-long pursuit of knowing God. ▼

Baptism does, however, continue the snowball effect Jesus started when He was baptized. If you want to make a difference in your walk with Christ, enter into a relationship with Him. If you have already done that, talk to your youth leader about following Jesus in baptism. If you have already done that, keep telling people Jesus is the Son of God, and that He came to save them from their sins.

04. Tested, Tried, and Triumphant

 Luke 4:1-13

MEMORY VERSE

All Scripture is God-breathed and is useful for teaching, rebuking, correcting and training in righteousness, so that the man of God may be thoroughly equipped for every good work.

2 Timothy 3:16-17

A Powerful Opponent—A More Powerful Friend

When Michael Jordan was still playing basketball, he was once asked how he got to be the world's best basketball player. He responded, "I played against the best competition available on a regular basis."

In what activities do you do your best?

❏ Sports ❏ Academics ❏ Friendships

❏ Cheerleading ❏ Music ❏ Drama

❏ Speech/Debate ❏ Student Government ❏ Volunteer/Service

❏ Other: _____

Think about your spiritual life. In resisting temptation, who is your strongest opponent? _____ How can standing against him make you better at resisting temptation?

35
Jesus and Temptations

From whom does your strongest support come? _____

How can your strongest supporter make you better at resisting temptation?

Satan is a powerful enemy. His desire to tempt you can work to your advantage if it causes you to stay close to Christ. Better yet, Christians have the most powerful friend in the universe. Christ can help you overcome your temptation. ❨

Christ's Temptations

Jesus had just been baptized. He had seen the Spirit of God descending onto Him as a dove. He had heard His Father's voice affirming Him. Would you agree this was a high point in Jesus' life?

Immediately afterward, Jesus went into the wilderness and was tempted. If Satan could cause Jesus to sin at the outset of His ministry, nothing else would matter. During the 40 days Jesus was tempted, He didn't eat. Perhaps He fasted to keep His mind fixed on His Father, God. At the end of the 40 days, Luke tells us Satan tempted Jesus in three more ways. Pay close attention because Satan will try the same tricks to tempt you. Read Luke 4:1-13.

Temptation #1—A Hungry Man Offered Bread (Luke 4:1-4)

After fasting for 40 days, this would have been an easy temptation for Jesus to give into. Satan will always try to use your own needs to tempt you. The problem is not that you don't have real needs. The problem is God does not want you to attempt to meet those needs outside of His plan. This is true of physical appetites like food. It is also true for needs like the need to be loved, the need to be happy, or the need to have purpose. God's desire is for you to have all of those needs met in ways He has provided. 🐾 When Jesus said, "Man does not live by bread alone," what did He mean?

Are there needs in your life Satan uses to tempt you to meet apart from God's plan? If so, what are they?

Temptation #2—Easy Path to Power (Luke 4:5-8)

In the end, Jesus is going to be the ruler of the universe. What was Satan offering Jesus that wasn't already His?

Satan was asking Jesus to compromise on what was right. He suggested Jesus could be the King without going through the pain of the cross. ▼ That would have been a difficult temptation for Jesus. Satan will also entice you to compromise. What are some compromises with which Satan tempts you?

Temptation #3—Prove Who You Are (Luke 4:9-12)

What might appeal to Jesus in this temptation?

God expected Jesus to risk everything to be faithful. God did not expect Jesus to risk recklessly to gain popularity. When Jesus said, "Do not put the Lord your God to the test," what did He mean?

Stones to Bread—After fasting for 40 days, Jesus would have been very hungry. The desert was full of little round pieces of limestone that looked much like little loaves of bread. It probably wasn't very hard for Satan to point out those stones and tempt Jesus to use His divine power to change them into bread. To do so would have been to use the power of God to meet His own physical needs. Instead, Jesus trusted God to provide food at the right time.

Highest Point of the Temple—The temple stood on top of Mount Zion. The top of the mountain was flattened into a plateau. The entire temple was on the plateau. At one corner, Solomon's Porch and the Royal Porch met. At that corner, there was a 450-foot drop to the Kedron Valley below. People would have surely been impressed if Jesus were to jump from that height and land unhurt.

Satan will tempt you to create a name for yourself. What do you think is the difference between honoring God with your life and doing great things to gain honor for yourself?

In what ways are you tempted to gain popularity or make a name for yourself?

Jesus' Battle Plan

Jesus withstood three powerful temptations in this passage. How did He do it? He used two battle tactics we must also use to win in our own battles against temptation.

Battle Tactic 1—He stayed close to God.
- He had just followed the Lord's will in baptism.
- He followed up that obedience by isolating Himself to get focused on pursuing God's will in His ministry.
- During this personal retreat, Satan stepped up to attempt to sidetrack God's plans for Jesus.

Battle Tactic 2—He knew God's Word.
- Jesus declined each temptation because pleasing God was His priority.
- Jesus battled each temptation by properly using God's Word.
- Even when Satan tried to distort God's Word, Jesus battled back with a proper use of memorized Scripture.

What About You?

What is one temptation you are facing? _____

Battle Tactic 1: How can you stay close to God?

Battle Tactic 2: How can you use God's Word to fight this particular temptation?

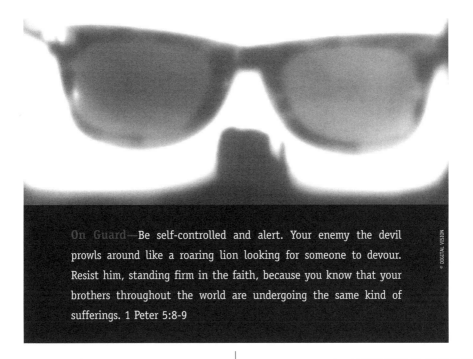

On Guard—Be self-controlled and alert. Your enemy the devil prowls around like a roaring lion looking for someone to devour. Resist him, standing firm in the faith, because you know that your brothers throughout the world are undergoing the same kind of sufferings. 1 Peter 5:8-9

DIGITAL VISION

Satan Retreats for a While

Temptation tests our heart for God.

1. If we give in to temptation, it reveals how deeply we need Christ on a daily basis.

2. If we resist temptation, it reveals how deeply we need Christ, because it is His power in us that helps us overcome temptation.

Read Luke 4:13 again. If you win your battle against temptation today, you cannot drop your guard. You must stay alert. Your adversary, the devil is waiting for an opportune time to sidetrack you spiritually. You must remain clear-minded and alert to his tactics.

 BEYOND THE BASICS!

- Memorize 2 Timothy 3:16-17.
- Interview 5 people who are very successful at what they do. Ask them what stumbling blocks they have to avoid to stay successful. Share with them you wish to be successful in pursuing God's will for your life. Ask them if they can apply lessons from their own success stories to help you create a game plan to fulfill God's purposes for your life.
- Create a Scripture memory list. Step up to the challenge of memorizing one entire chapter of the Bible. James 1 or Romans 6 are great chapters to memorize.

05. Following the Call

 Matthew 4:18-22, 9:9-13

MEMORY VERSE

"Come, follow me," Jesus said, "and I will make you fishers of men."

Matthew 4:19

It's Hard to Say Goodbye

Change is always difficult. It's especially hard when you have become accustomed to a certain lifestyle. Michael Jordon first entered the NBA® in 1984. While he was there, he enjoyed unparalleled success. He won three NBA championships with the Chicago Bulls. He was named Most Valuable Player three times. He played in nine All-Star games. He signed multi-million dollar deals with sporting goods companies. He had arguably the greatest professional basketball career in history.

When he retired the first time in 1993, it didn't take. He missed the game. He missed the thrill of winning. Though he looked forward to retirement, what he found there was different than what he left behind. He had to come back. His experience was similar to many professional athletes following their retirements. It is a tough transition to move from something you know and love to a radically new lifestyle.

Jesus called a group of men out of the only lifestyle they had ever known. They made a drastic choice and left many things behind. Evidence suggests they sometimes wondered if it was worth it (Matt. 19:27). The fishermen were doing the same thing they had done for countless days before that day. Then suddenly a man showed up out of nowhere and said simply, "Follow me." That's a pretty bold command from someone they barely knew. But what is even more amazing is the response of the fishermen: they left their boats, their nets, the water, and followed Him—*immediately*.

Having Your Life Changed

Every day is not a life-changing day. However, all of us can look back at some significant days in our lives. In the space provided, jot down significant days you can remember, days when your life changed.

Read Matthew 4:18-22 and 9:9-13. Pay particular attention to Jesus' request and the disciples' responses. The first aspect of the call to be a disciple is that Jesus initiates it, and it is an invitation to salvation. In the passages you just read, note the disciples didn't initiate the call. In the Jewish culture of the day, a man would choose a rabbi from whom he wanted to learn and then become that rabbi's disciple. This is not the way Jesus' disciples came to Him. Jesus personally chose them to be His disciples. ▼

The second aspect of the call was that Jesus called them to a new purpose and identity; this was part of their commissioning. Jesus said they would no longer be fishermen, but fishers of men. Their purpose was not simply to follow Jesus around; they were called to be disciples. They were to learn from Jesus and practice the things they learned.

A Radical Call—Matthew 4:22 says the disciples left the boat "and their father" and followed Jesus. In that day there were no assisted living or nursing homes. Families were very tightly knit, and adult children were expected to care for their aging parents. The call of Christ was not only to leave their occupation; He called them to abandon the social customs with which they were comfortable and simply follow Him. In reality, the call to follow Him will always cause us to leave some things behind.

Tax Collector—The Roman government who ruled over the Jews at that time had many different forms of taxes. They would tax:
- Goods traveling in and out of the city,
- People crossing bridges,
- Land people owned,
- Young people who turned fourteen years old.

Most tax collectors collecting from Jewish people were Jews enlisted by the government. Their payment came from whatever they collected above the amount required by government. Tax collectors overcharged people and pocketed the extra cash for themselves. Most became very wealthy. The Jewish people viewed them as thieves and traitors. Jesus' call to Matthew meant he would begin a radically different life.

In the space provided, jot down what comes into your mind when you think of the American Dream?

Some would think of lots of money. Others think of a college education. Still others think of a great job. But all of those ideas can be summed up pretty simply: you can accomplish anything if you try hard enough. Haven't you heard that before? People say these types of things: "Be all you can be," "Just put your mind to it," and "Don't settle for second best."

For the most part, those things are true. However, they are only true because American society allows you to advance yourself. It was not that way in the first century. During that time, there was very little movement between life stations. A slave would always be a slave and his children would also be slaves. A farmer would always be a farmer and his children would also be farmers. A fisherman would always be a fisherman and his children would also be fisherman.

When Jesus said "follow me," He was asking for a lot more than allegiance. He was asking His followers to abandon their whole way of life. They had to leave their occupations. They had to leave their sources of income. They even had to leave their families.

What Does It All Mean?

Though you may have never had to make such a drastic change, following Christ still requires sacrifice. Take some time to list some of the things you have had to leave behind in order to follow Jesus. How did these sacrifices affect your life?

The call to obedience was immediate. The invitation to follow Him wasn't an open-ended invitation. He didn't say, whenever you feel like it, come on. There was timeliness to His call. The Bible says they "*at once* left their nets and followed him." Fishing was their livelihood and they left it behind. Luke 5:11 says they "left everything." This same truth was evident in Matthew's call. In Matthew 9:9, Matthew left his booth as a **tax collector** when Jesus called him to follow Him.

Fishermen, Fish!

Jesus could have given His disciples any command. But He told them if they followed Him, He would make them fishers of men. But in fishing, they had already learned important lessons that would help them in their ministry. They knew the right timing of fishing. They had learned how to work as a team. They had learned the persistence and patience necessary to have an effective catch. 👥

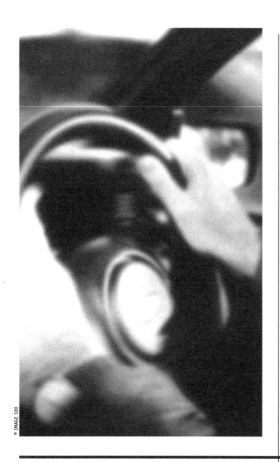

© IMAGE 100

Your Response

Jesus calls people from all kinds of vocations to serve Him. This may or may not mean leaving their job, but it does mean a total commitment of life. Next to each profession below, jot ways God can use it to reach people. The first one is completed for you.

Teacher—Teach the Bible to people

Athlete _____

Actor _____

Investor _____

Architect_____

Writer/Editor_____

Scientist_____

Doctor _____

Musician _____

Artist/Designer_____

So how about you? Do you play basketball? Do drama? Play an instrument? God wants to use you in the middle of your world to reach others. He told the fishermen, "Go fish." What is He telling you?

BEYOND THE BASICS!

- Memorize Matthew 4:19.
- What is "your world"? Make a list of your different activities for a week. Then make a list of people God can use you to reach that also participate in those activities.
- Write a description of your own calling. Include what you were called away from and what Jesus is commanding you to do.

Following the Call

by Michael Kelley

"Come, follow me." Now there's a command that raises some questions: "Follow you? Why should I?" "Follow you and do what?" Or better yet: "Okay, I'll follow – but where?" God has a habit of putting out the call without answering all the questions. At least that's how He did it with Abraham in Genesis 12: "Leave your homeland." That's it. He didn't say where or how or what specifically the journey would entail – just go. And it didn't stop with Abraham.

He told Moses, "So now, go. I am sending you to Pharaoh to bring my people the Israelites out of Egypt" (Ex. 3:10). But that still left a lot of questions: "How will you do that?" "What if they won't listen?" "But I can't even speak very well!" And the pattern continued. Whether it was Jeremiah the prophet, David the king, Andrew the fisherman, or Matthew the tax collector, God extended the call without disclosing the entire plan.

As followers of Christ, we have heard the same call: "Come. Go. Leave. Believe. Follow." Oh sure, we know there is an inheritance waiting for us in heaven, but it's a long journey to that destination. We too have many questions. Like those men and women of the past, we don't know the details of the journey.

Did you ever go on family vacations as a kid? My family did; we went just about everywhere. We went to the Grand Canyon; Washington, D.C.; Los Angeles; Las Vegas; Colorado; New Mexico; Virginia; and just about everywhere in between. A vacation for us was more than getting to a destination; it was about the journey. We would pass through countless cities, numerous highway construction zones, several detours, and dozens of rest stops on our way to where we were going. What great memories those are!

The funny thing is that, as a kid, I knew a lot about the destination, but not so much about the journey. I didn't know when we needed to get gas or which hotel we would stay at. I didn't know when to exit off of the Interstate or when to get back on. But my dad did. And because he knew, I didn't have to know all the details.

Our whole lives are a journey, a journey with many unanswered questions. We'll never know all the details. But the One we follow does. He will not lead us astray. He is our biggest ally. Because of Him, we are able to accept the uncertainty.

We don't know exactly where we are going or what we will be doing, but we certainly know what we are leaving. Abraham had to leave his homeland. Peter, Andrew, James, and John had to leave their occupation and their families. Moses had to leave the life he was accustomed to in the wilderness. God's call will affect many parts of your life. It affects you as you choose a college. It affects you as you decide whether or not to participate in sports for your school. It affects you as you choose who to date. It affects you in regard to your families, interests, fears, and worries.

At first glance, this call may seem heartless, or too strict. We can try to dance around Jesus' words all day long, but He meant it when He said, "Anyone who loves his father or mother more than me is not worthy of me; anyone who loves his son or daughter more than me is not worthy of me; and anyone who does not take his cross and follow me is not worthy of me," (Matthew 10:37-38). What kind of leader would place such radical demands on His followers, calling people away from everything they know and love? The answer? The *best* kind of leader! If God did anything less than this, He would not really love us.

I used to love fast food hamburgers. McDonald's™, Wendy's™, Burger King™—it didn't matter much because a hamburger was a hamburger, and I loved them all. To me, the best piece of meat imaginable was one of those thin patties slapped between a bun with a little mustard. Then the day came when I first ate prime rib. What was this? Some new kind of meat? Something you actually have to use a fork to eat? And the taste—unbelievable. That changed the way I approached food forever. I had tasted the best, and now somehow those hamburgers had lost their luster.

If we keep on reading that Scripture in Matthew 10, we see Jesus has more to say after He calls His followers to abandon everything. He says that in doing this, even though you are abandoning your former life, you are actually finding your true life. God wants you to live the most fulfilling life imaginable, but the road you have to walk to get there is one of abandonment. When we release everything and follow God wholeheartedly, we find that the joy far exceeds what we left behind. It is as if we have tasted prime rib. We look back at hamburger and can scarcely believe we held it so dear.

However, when you leave your circumstances they don't leave you. Think about the way Jesus called those first disciples. He said to them, "Follow me, and I will make you fishers of men" (Matt. 10:19). Notice Jesus didn't forget the disciples' experiences before they became disciples. Before they were disciples, they were fishermen. Much in the same way, God wants to use all your experiences, all your upbringing, all your knowledge, all your talents, and even all your pain and disappointment. God allowed the previous circumstances into your life. He has created the way you look. He has chosen the town and family where you find yourself. Now He wants to bring all those things together as you discover what He has chosen for you to be involved in. So don't be afraid. God knows you better than you know yourself. Follow Him, though you may not know where, and you will truly find your life.

06. Don't Worry About It

 Matthew 6:19-34

© DIGITAL VISION

MEMORY VERSE

Who of you by worrying can

add a single hour to his life?

Matthew 6:27

Blessed Are the Who?

Can you picture the scene in your mind? Jesus had traveled throughout the region stopping in the smaller towns and had developed a reputation as a great teacher. But He was also healing people and driving out demons. People had begun to talk:

"You'll never believe what I saw Him do. He made my cousin walk again."

"Yeah? That's nothing! I saw Him heal a man that was born blind!"

"I heard He's the next king of the Jews!"

Yep, the rumor mill was really running. Jesus had acquired such a reputation that large crowds had followed Him to a mountain. There He started to teach. He was at the peak of His popularity and everyone wanted to hear Him. But His words were surprising.

Blessing—For centuries people believed God's blessing always came in the form of tangible, material benefits. People thought it was easy in the first century to see who was blessed. The blessed were the richest people with the most animals and the biggest families. Jesus turned the idea of blessing on its head. Blessing is not about material benefits. In fact, Jesus said the poor, sad, humble, hungry, and thirsty are blessed. What a reversal!

© DIGITAL VISION

Christ in all things—When we become Christians, we suddenly have a new home in heaven. But even though that is our true home, we still must live here. So we are to bring that heavenly focus to our everyday activities in this world.

Go back and re-read Matthew 5:1-12. If you're like me, when you think of "**blessing**" you think of something good, something a person would want to have. "I'm blessed with good looks," or "I got a check for $1,000! What a blessing!" Jesus' view of being "blessed" seems different. What surprises you about the people Jesus called "blessed"?

Investment Strategies from Jesus

Do you have a savings account for college? You may be saving money in a mutual fund or a money market fund. You probably haven't started saving for retirement yet, but your parents may have an IRA, a 401K, or some other retirement savings plan. If so, they are putting money aside for their future.

Jesus has an investment strategy for believers. One day we will all retire, and Jesus, as our Investment Counselor, wants to make sure we have all we need for that day. For this reason, He lines out a sound investment strategy in Matthew 6:19-24.

Read Matthew 6:19-24 in your Bible. 👥

It's a great plan. But just like an earthly retirement plan, it will mean some hard choices.

Your Treasure

How many hours a week do you spend playing sports? How about studying? What about watching television and movies? Do you spend any time practicing an instrument or an activity like drama? Examining your time is a good way to tell what it is you really treasure. You spend time doing what is most important to you. Jesus wants to make sure your priorities are in the right place.

So what if there is something we treasure more than God? What if it is school, sports, or even our families? Does Jesus want us to stop doing those things?

In some cases, God does want us to give up certain things in our lives, especially if we are involved in sin. God wants to be the most important thing in our lives. It's not that we have to stop playing sports, practicing the trumpet, or watching movies. We just need to be sure our main focus is God's will. The key lies in our motivation. GOD

Is it possible to honor God on the football field, the basketball court, or in the band room? How about in the classroom, after school with your friends, or on the job? What can you do to accomplish this?

Source of Worry

Many people think a lack of material things causes worry. People who are very poor definitely have significant challenges. However, some are often generous with what they have and not terribly concerned about where money will come from. Some rich people are full of anxiety about their money, their business, their stuff, and their lives.

Leo Tolstoy wrote about a woman who lost all her wealth in his novel, *Elias*.

> "When we were rich, my husband and I had so many cares we had no time to talk to one another, or to think of our souls or to pray to God," she explained … "Now, when my husband and I wake up in the morning, we always have a loving word for one another, and we live peacefully, having nothing to quarrel about."

What do you think creates worry?

In Matthew 6:25 Jesus said there was a relationship between worrying and where people had placed their treasure. Most people worry about their stuff. They worry about whether or not they will have enough money for the future. They worry about the size of their house. They worry about their stocks. But those things, like most other things, are simply out of their control.

The Cure

The cure for worry is definitely not possessions. Jesus' logic was simple in Matthew 6:25-34. The solution to worry is trusting the One who has control. So many circumstances are out of your control. If you were not sure of God's love, there would be no reason for you to trust Him. You would never know whether or not situations would work out for the best.

But you can be completely sure of God's love for you. So not only do you know the One who is in control of the whole universe, you can be sure He always has your best interests at heart. In light of this, it almost seems silly to worry.

Write Matthew 6:27 on a small sheet of paper and put it in your back pocket. Commit to reading this verse this week every time you begin to worry about something.

What do you worry about?

How can you trust God for what you need?

BEYOND THE BASICS!

- Memorize Matthew 6:27.
- Make a list of the top five things that worry you. Rewrite Matthew 6:25-27 by inserting these five worries. Then write out prayers of confidence that confess God's ability to take care of those situations.
- Volunteer to work in the yard or clean the house of an elderly neighbor. Don't accept any payment for the work.
- Go back and reread the entire Sermon on the Mount once a day for the next 5 days. Each day journal about a specific section that is meaningful to you.

07

Answering the **Ultimate** Question

 Mark 8:27-33

MEMORY VERSE

"But what about you?" he asked.

"Who do you say I am?" Peter

answered, "You are the Christ."

Mark 8:29

© PHOTODISC

The Rumor Mill

Have you every played the game gossip? That's the game where everyone sits in a circle, and one person whispers a message to another person. That person then whispers it to the next person, and so on. It's always funny to see just how distorted the message gets by the time it makes it all the way around the circle.

People are like that, aren't they? When the rumor mill starts running, things can quickly get out of control. Think about all the things that happened since Jesus called His first disciples. Let's check out the progress that was made:

Location	Event	Scripture
Capernaum	Jesus chose the 12 disciples	Mark 3:13-19
Capernaum	Jesus preached the Sermon on the Mount	Matthew 5:1-7:29
Galilee	Jesus preached throughout Galilee	Matthew 13:1-52
Sea of Galilee	Jesus calmed the storm	Matthew 8:23-27

Location	Event	Scripture
Capernaum	Jesus raised Jairus's daughter from the dead	Matthew 9:18-26
Capernaum	Jesus sent His 12 followers out to preach and heal	Matthew 9:35-11:1
Near Bethsaida	Jesus walked on water	Matthew 14:22-33
Tyre/Sidon	Jesus fed 4,000 people	Matthew 15:32-39

People had been healed. Great sermons had been preached. Wonderful miracles had been done. Jesus had been building quite a reputation. As you can guess, the rumor mill was really running, and people were asking, "Who is this man?" Read Mark 8:27-33 and identify the many different ideas people had about who Jesus was.

A Case of Mistaken Identity

There were many different ideas about Jesus' identity during His time. Mark 8:27-28 says Jesus asked His disciples an important question about His perceived identity: "Who do people say I am?" The disciples give a few different answers. They told Him some said John the Baptist, others said Elijah, and still others Jeremiah or one of the prophets. In those days, to be compared to any or all of these historical characters would have been a huge complement. The people were impressed by this man named Jesus.

Jot down why you think people would say those things about Jesus.

The fact is, Jesus was not really concerned about who the crowds thought He was; He was more concerned about who individuals thought He was. In Mark 8:29, Jesus said, Okay, okay, so that's who all *those* people say I am, but what about you? Who do you say I am?

What about you? Who do you say Jesus is?

The Foundation of Faith

Peter was sure about Jesus' identity. His declaration was bold and powerful: "You are the **Christ**." It is important to realize that Peter's statement is the foundation for our faith. Make no mistake. Your personal relationship with Jesus starts with this statement of faith. Have you come to a point where you have made a similar declaration? Like Peter you must lay aside what others say about Jesus and wrap your mind around His true identity, making this the foundation of your faith. ▼

Not There Yet

Read Mark 8:30. Jesus' response to Peter's declaration was strange at the very least. Why would He tell His disciples not to tell anyone about His identity? Wasn't that the point? Didn't He want to equip His disciples to tell others about Him? The reason for His strange instructions becomes clear in the next few verses when He began to speak of His coming suffering and death. The disciples didn't need to speak about what they still did not understand completely.

Christ—When Jesus asked the disciples who they believed He was, it was Peter who spoke up. "You are the Christ," Peter said. The word literally means, "anointed one." The Old Testament Scriptures had foretold of the coming of a King who would be a descendent of King David. He would redeem His people from their sins. In Jesus' day, most Jews believed the Messiah would be a conquering King who would drive out the Romans. It is doubtful that even the disciples understood the Messiah would die for the sins of the world, as the next few verses reveal.

Caesarea Philippi—Caesarea Philippi lies about 25 miles northeast of the Sea of Galilee. (Locate it on the map on page 49.) The population was mainly non-Jewish, and there Jesus would have peace to teach the Twelve. Few locations had more religious implications than this place. It was a mystical place scattered with temples of ancient Syrian Baal worship. Near the city, there was a great hill with a deep cavern said to be the birthplace of the great god Pan, the god of nature. In fact, the original name of the place was Panias after the god. This cave was said to be where the sources of the Jordan sprang to life. In Caesarea Philippi, there was a great temple of white marble, built to the godhead of Caesar, which dominated the landscape. The fact that Jesus, the Son of God, asked the ordinary men who were following Him to come to terms with His identity at this historically religious place is a compelling fact. ⊤

Read Mark 8:31-33. It is amazing that Peter could make such a clear and insightful observation of Jesus' identity and then almost with his next breath stumble into an inappropriate understanding of Christ's purpose. When Jesus began to speak of His upcoming days of suffering and death, it just didn't fit the disciples' definition of the "Christ." As usual, Peter spoke up. He pulled Jesus aside and directed Him not to talk like that. He probably argued that these were not the words of the Messiah they had been expecting.

Peter's misunderstanding earned him a stern rebuke from Jesus. Jesus told Peter he was thinking from a secular perspective rather than a spiritual one. Peter's words contradicted his own statement of faith a few minutes earlier. In fact, Jesus' language was similar to what He used with Satan when He was tempted in the wilderness.

Have you struggled with the same kind of thinking in your life? Write down some times when you have had some inappropriate expectations of God. 🏃

Your Response

Life has many parts. Everyday we engage in situations with school, classmates, family, friends, and teammates. We make choices about whom we will date, what we will study, and what our career will be. In a way, all of those situations and decisions are like building a house. We are the architects, and every day we draw the blueprints of what the house of our lives will look like.

Spend some time thinking about your life. Are you centered on making money? Is your life built on the desire for popularity? There is only one lasting foundation, and that is Jesus. On what are you building your life? List the things that are the foundation that gives structure to every part of your life.

The foundation of a high-rise building is extremely significant to anchor the weight and structure of the building. The Empire State Building in New York is 102 stories tall (1,454 ft.). The foundation for that building is five stories deep (55 ft.). Not only that but the foundation covers 79,288 square feet or almost two acres. That's almost 55 times the height. Foundations are significant in our lives as well. We must begin with the confession that Christ is the Son of the Living God.

 BEYOND THE BASICS!

- Memorize Mark 8:29.
- Read about some of Peter's later life decisions in John 18:15-27; Acts 2:1-41; Acts 4:1-22; Acts 10. Write a short biography of how Peter's confession influenced his life.
- Build on the foundation of Christ by visiting a local nursing home and offering to give a devotion for the residents who live there.
- Look for a place where you can serve in your local church and volunteer to help in that area of ministry.

08

Seeing Christ for **Who** He Is

 Matthew 17:1-13

MEMORY VERSE

While he was still speaking, a bright cloud

enveloped them, and a voice from the cloud

said, "This is my Son, whom I love; with

him I am well pleased. Listen to him."

Matthew 17:5

© DIGITAL VISION

Metamorphosis

Have you ever seen the movie, *The Wizard of Oz*? For the first half hour, the movie is in black and white film. Everything looks very drab and grey. But then comes the scene in the movie where the tornado hits the farm and transports the farmhouse to Oz. When Dorothy emerges from the house, everything is in color. The flowers, the trees, and the people—everything looks so much more radiant and vibrant than it did before.

Something a little like that happened with Jesus on a mountaintop. Read Matthew 17:1-13. There they were—Peter, James, John, and Jesus. Everything was normal. Suddenly, Jesus was changed or **transfigured** before their eyes. He was shining like the sun! They could see a glimpse of His glory. It was like they had lived their whole lives in black and white but suddenly everything had gone to color right before their very eyes. They couldn't look away from Jesus. But Jesus was not alone. ▼

Imagine yourself on that mountain with Jesus. As you wrote about your experience in your journal later, what would you say?

Meeting a Hero

In 1999, goalie Eddie Belfour led the Dallas Stars to win the Stanley Cup, the National Hockey League's highest award. Now playing for the Toronto Maple Leaves, Eddie is known as one of the all-time leading goalies. That probably was the reason why he was Kyle's hero. As Eddie was playing for the Dallas

Transfigured—The Greek word Matthew used was *metamorphoo*, which means to change into another form. He described this transformation as Jesus' face becoming bright as the sun and His clothes being extremely white. The voice from heaven later confirmed this was indeed a picture of Jesus' glory. "This is my Son, whom I love; with him I am well pleased. Listen to him!" (Matt. 17:5)

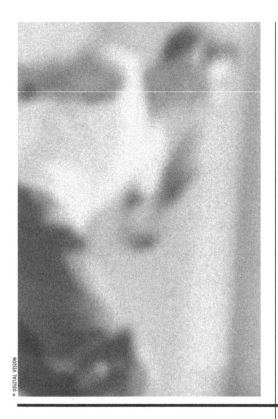

© DIGITAL VISION

Moses—Few people in the history of Israel held as high a place as Moses. Moses was the instrument God used to deliver His people out of slavery in Egypt (Exodus 7-12) and parted the Red Sea (Exodus 13). But his most important contribution came in Exodus 20-31 when God gave Moses the law to give to the nation of Israel. These were the commandments that defined the Jews as a people. It is hard to overstate the importance of the law to Israel. Needless to say, Moses was much revered as the one who had delivered it. Additionally, Jewish tradition held that Moses would return to announce the coming of the Messiah.

Stars, nine-year-old Kyle was playing for his local hockey team, the Hawks ... despite his battle with cystic fibrosis. Kyle played goalie just like Eddie. When the Make-a-Wish Foundation® heard about Kyle's struggle with this life threatening disease and his determination, they met with him. The Make-a-Wish Foundation grants "wishes" to children with life-threatening medical conditions. Kyle's wish was easy. He wanted to meet his hero, Eddie Belfour.

Kyle and his family were treated to special seating at a game to watch Eddie and the Stars beat the Ottawa Senators. Later, he was given a VIP tour of the Stars locker room where he met Eddie and the rest of the stars team. Belfour spent time with Kyle and even offered him goal-tending tips. Later, when Kyle logged onto Eddie's Website, he found that Eddie had written about meeting Kyle and his brother Derek. He had written, "They are both great kids. It was a lot of fun playing and knowing you guys were in the stands cheering for me." When he read that, Kyle's face lit up. It was like he got the wish all over again.

Who are your heroes in life? If you could meet anyone, whom would you want to meet?

A Holy Huddle

Everybody has heroes. The heroes of Israel were the people they heard about in the synagogue and read about in the Scriptures. Their heroes were people like Abraham, King David, and Queen Esther. But no one held with more honor than **Moses** and **Elijah**. Moses was the giver of the law. Elijah was the greatest prophet.

What do you think they would be talking to Jesus about on that mountain? Matthew doesn't tell us, but read Luke's account of this event in Luke 9:28-36. What does Luke say they were talking about? Write what you discover here:

The word departure is "exodus" in Greek. It is the same word used when God led His people out of Egypt. Just like in the days of the Exodus, God was about to free His people again. The first time, He freed them from slavery. This time He would free them from sin. The first time He freed them from the

Elijah—If Moses was the greatest lawgiver, then Elijah was considered the greatest prophet. Throughout 1 and 2 Kings, Elijah stood in the face of persecution. He fought against evil King Ahab and his conniving wife, Jezebel. He performed many miracles including raising a widow's son from the dead (1 Kings 17). He met with God on top of a mountain just as Moses did (1 Kings 19). His greatest victory came when he challenged 450 prophets of Baal to a contest. The God of Israel prevailed and Elijah triumphed over the enemies of the Lord. At the end of his life, Elijah was taken up into heaven by a chariot of fire (2 Kings 2). The Jews believed the prophesy of Malachi 4:5 that said Elijah would return before the day of the Lord.

Egyptians. This time He would free them death. The second exodus was about to occur, and Jesus would be the deliverer this time. The exodus would be His death. ☨

The Best Day

What was the best day of your life? Describe it here:

- Memorize Matthew 17:5.
- Do a study of the different accounts of the transfiguration in Matthew 17, Mark 9, Luke 9. Make a list of the similarities and differences.
- Ask four senior members of your church to describe some of their most significant mountaintop experiences with Christ.

© DIGITAL VISION

Put yourself in Peter's position. What a day he was having! He had been a witness to the glory of Christ. It's pretty obvious why Peter wanted to stay. In fact, he offered to build shelters for everyone. Before he could finish his suggestion, he heard a voice that reminded him his job was to listen—not to speak. "This is my Son. I am proud of Him. Listen to what He says." Difficult days were coming. The cross was before Jesus and the disciples. But Peter could not live life on the mountaintop. As good as that day was, Peter had to come down and follow Jesus to the cross.

You have great days ahead of you. There will times on top of the mountain when things are wonderful spiritually. But there are some difficult days ahead too. You cannot live on top of the mountain. Your job is not to stay on top; it is simply to follow Jesus.

Are you on the mountain or in the valley today? Regardless of where you are, write a fresh commitment to follow your Lord here:

Leading Like Jesus

by Dwayne C. Ulmer

The Yellow Jersey

The Tour de France® is the biggest sporting event in the world, outside of the World Cup® and the Olympic Games®. Since the Tour began in 1903 there have been 90 races with 54 different winners. The race lasts three weeks, covers 3,462 kilometers throughout France, and has 20 stages not including the prologue on the first day. Shortly after World War I, the race introduced the "yellow jersey." It was awarded to the rider who was leading the race after each stage. The first man who won it refused to wear it believing it singled him out as a target for his opponents. Since that time, the jersey has become a symbol of excellence and leadership within the cycling community. It is the goal of every rider to pursue the yellow jersey in hopes of owning it on the last day of the race.

Wouldn't you love to wear a yellow jersey? Maybe not in the Tour de France, but don't you want to be the best at something? Within each of us there is a desire to step to the front and make our mark on the world. Christians are called to be leaders. It's easy to misunderstand what God's call of leadership really means. Leadership, very simply, is influence. If you have influence over another person, you are a leader. There are many ways to influence. You don't have to be the captain of the team, first chair in the band, an officer in student government, or have the lead in the school play to have influence.

The Model Leader

Of all the leaders who have ever led, Jesus Christ stands out as the ultimate. When He put on His "yellow jersey," it not only made Him a target for His enemies but it also made Him the perfect model for those He was called to lead. Ironically, He never wrote a book, led an army, or was elected to public office. He wasn't a famous athlete or musician and never appeared on television or film. Yet, from the beginning, humanity has contemplated how to respond to His influence. His name is associated with greatness and His life exemplifies perfect leadership. A closer look at Christ's life can provide insight for you as you discover how and where God has called you to lead. Jesus led with the right heart, He influenced people with His head and mind, He performed leadership with His hands, and He sustained leadership with His habits.

The Heart

Jesus had the heart of a servant. This may seem to contradict everything we associate with leadership, but it remains the foundational principle of leading. In his letter to the Philippians, Paul challenged us to follow Jesus' example (Phil. 2:5-8). Likewise, Jesus told His disciples, "whoever wants to be first must be your slave—just as the Son of Man did not come to be served, but to serve, and to give his life as a ransom for many" (Matt. 20:28). Authentic and effective leadership is built on service. When you have opportunity to influence others, it is important you consider their benefit first. As soon as you come to understand this concept, you will be well on your way to becoming a leader.

The Head

The head is the center of knowledge. All leaders have a point of view that defines how they see their role. Their knowledge must be grounded in a vision of the future that excites passion and inspires commitment in those who follow. This vision contains a purpose or mission—your picture of the future (where you are going and what you are trying to accomplish) and your values (what you stand for). Jesus' vision was given to Him by His Father and it included expanding the kingdom of God through the discipleship of all nations (Matt. 28:19).

The Hands

Servants who are leaders do something. James 1:22 says, "Do not merely listen to the word and so deceive yourselves. Do what it says." Paul told the Colossians, "Whatever you do, work at it with all your heart, as working for the Lord and not for men" (Col. 3:23). Good leaders will follow the example of Christ and act according to the needs of those they are leading. Effective leaders see the situation, evaluate it, and then adapt their leadership styles to assist those they are leading to accomplish the goal.

The Habits

The character of an effective leader will reflect the character of Christ. Before character traits can be established, habits must be implemented. Before habits can be implemented, a person must first practice them as disciplines. Without adequate character and habits, the daily pressure of leadership will erode the long-term effectiveness of the leader. There are several key habits Jesus modeled for His followers. Teenagers can easily begin to fold them into their lives. They are:

- Solitude—time alone with God;
- Prayer—speaking with God;
- Storing up God's Word—memorizing Scripture and maintaining personal Bible study;
- Faith in God's Unconditional Love—proceeding with confi-

dence grounded in trust; and
- Involvement in Accountability Relationships—sharing His vulnerability.

All of these are evident throughout the life of Christ. The key to success is making them a part of your lifestyle and embedding them into your character.

Put on the Yellow Jersey

God has gifted you with a yellow jersey if you have made Him the Lord of your life. He expects you to step up and lead a pack of followers. When you put on the jersey, you will become a target for the enemy but you will also become an example for others to find their way. Remember, effective leadership begins with servanthood and ends with trust in the ultimate leader, Christ, who lives inside you.

Note: Feature was heavily influenced by the work of Ken Blanchard and Phil Hodges in *The Servant Leader: Transforming Your Heart, Head, Hands, and Habits,* Nashville, TN: Countryman, 2003.

09.At Your Service

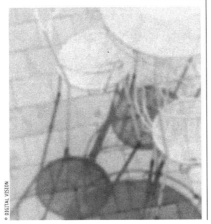

© DIGITAL VISION

MEMORY VERSE

Sitting down, Jesus called the Twelve and said, "If anyone wants to be first, he must be the very last, and the servant of all."

Mark 9:35

"The Greatest of All Time"

On February 25, 1964, the seven-to-one underdog Cassius Clay (later known as Mohammad Ali) defeated the Heavyweight Champion of the World, Sonny Liston. At the conclusion of the fight, Clay victoriously danced around the ring shouting to the skeptical journalists, "Who is the greatest? Eat your words! I shook up the world." A little over a year later he successfully defended his title against the same opponent setting in motion a career that would change the sport and elevate the boxer to icon status. Over the next 17 years, Ali would win the world title three times and successfully defend it 19 times ending his 20-year professional career with 56 wins (37 by knock out) and only five losses (plus an Olympic gold medal in 1960). He clearly earned the boxing title "The Greatest of All Time."[1]

But was Ali truly the greatest of all time? In the arena of boxing this may be so, but definitely not in life. Winning boxing titles doesn't make you the greatest. It doesn't even necessarily make you the greatest boxer.

All-Star Line Up!

Identify people who you think are the greatest in the following fields.

Basketball Player _____	**Boxer** _____
Pianist _____	**Comedian** _____
Biker _____	**Artist** _____
Golfer _____	**Soccer Player** _____
Homerun Hitter _____	**Running Back** _____
Pilot _____	**Composer** _____
Chef _____	**Magician** _____
Auto Racer _____	**Military General** _____
Singer _____	**Gymnast** _____

How do you know who is the greatest in a particular field? If you were to compare your responses with friends' would they be the same or different? Why is it possible to debate your choices?

Who Is the Greatest?

How would you describe someone who is great? List the top five characteristics that define greatness from the world's point of view, according to Scripture, and then from your point of view.

WORLD VIEW	GOD'S VIEW	MY VIEW

Read Mark 9:33-37. You will also want to read Matthew 18:1-4 and Luke 9:45-50. Jesus was just telling the disciples about His coming betrayal and murder. The next discussion Mark recorded was the disciples' argument over who was the greatest. The disciples totally missed God's view of greatness.

Think about the question Jesus asked the disciples, "What were you arguing about?" Don't you think He already knew? If so, why did He ask? Most likely He planned to turn their foolish argument into an opportunity to teach them about real greatness. We are too much like the disciples, too much like Mohammad Ali dancing around in the ring telling the world, "I'm the greatest of all time." Our arrogance only creates anger in others.

If You Want to Be First, You Have to Be Last

Look again at the story set in Capernaum. Mark gave us the account of Jesus asking the disciples about their discussion as they approached the town.

• What did Jesus say was the key to greatness?

• What object lesson did He use to make His point?

• Why do you think He chose this object?

The disciples were deathly silent when He asked the question. His powerful words shattered the silence, "If anyone wants to be first, he must be the very last, and the **servant** of all." That must have caught them by surprise. The words were a paradox. How could you be first and last or last and first?

Put a check in front of the qualities you believe are found in a servant.

❑ Willing   ❑ Loyal   ❑ Self-seeking   ❑ Humble   ❑ Selfish
❑ Teachable   ❑ Insignificant   ❑ Faithful   ❑ Powerful ❑ Influence
❑ High Society   ❑ Obedient   ❑ Arrogant   ❑ Gentle

A servant is willing, loyal, humble, teachable, faithful, obedient, and gentle. Which of these words define your life? _____

Would you rather be served or serve? Why?

A Child Will Teach Them

Read Mark 9:36-37 and Matthew 18:2-5. Jesus taught the disciples by calling a **child** to Himself. Their focus should not be on seeking position but on following their Master. Jesus was introducing the disciples to the qualities of a servant lifestyle. It begins by surrendering yourself to Christ's control. ❨

Jesus modeled a servant lifestyle. Look up the passages to the right. How are they examples of Christ's service? Write your responses beneath each.

The greatest is the one who places others first, the one who is more concerned about serving others than being served. Jesus modeled this as He told us how to live, washed the disciples' feet, fed a hungry crowd, and suffered and died for the sins of humankind. ⊤

Servant—Jesus used the Greek word *diakonos*. It is one of two major words for servant in the New Testament, the other being *doulos*, which had more of a "slave" meaning. This word has more of a "ministry" meaning. Jesus was saying that if you want to be great, you don't do so by seeking rank or position and the power that comes with it; you do it by seeking to minister to others.

Sermon on the Mount
Matthew 5:1-11

Towel & Water Basin
John 13:1-17

Feeding the Five Thousand
Matthew 15:29-37

The Crucifixion
Isaiah 53:3-6 and Mark 15

You Can't–God Can

How can you develop a life of service? First, you must surrender to Him. Then, allow God to begin the work of servanthood in your life. Watch for God to put people in your life you can serve. Are you expecting those opportunities? 🏃🏃

Child—In the Jewish culture of the day, children, although loved by their families, had absolutely no status or power. As far as society was concerned, children could do nothing to help its cause. In and of themselves, they were powerless in their society. Understanding this will help one properly interpret the point Jesus wanted to make to His disciples.

© IMAGE SOURCE

 BEYOND THE BASICS!

- Memorize Mark 9:35.
- Complete a topical, personal Bible study on the word "servant."
- List the characteristics that make the greatest Christian you know great. Circle the characteristics that involve service or ministry.
- Take a spiritual gifts inventory and discover what gifts the Holy Spirit has given you to use as you serve others. Your pastor or youth minister can assist you with the inventory.

You will have numerous opportunities to share Christ through your example of service. The true measure of greatness is service.

Your Response

Read the following scenarios and list possible ways to serve.

- Your youth group has had visitors coming. You have noticed that most visitors do not come back a second time.
- Mrs. Hernandez's husband died in September. He always loved working in his yard and kept it immaculate. You notice that the leaves are piling up and the flowerbeds need weeding.
- Some of the children who live down the street from your church have started attending Bible study and worship on Sundays. You overhear a couple of people complaining that the children do not know how to act in worship.
- Shiva and her family were in a car accident. She broke her right foot and left leg. She will be in the hospital for three weeks and then moved to a rehabilitation center.

1. See http://www.float-like-a-butterfly.de/indexe.htm.

P2: Prayer Points

 Matthew 6:9-13

MEMORY VERSE

This, then, is how you should pray: "Our Father in heaven, hallowed be your name, your kingdom come, your will be done on earth as it is in heaven. Give us today our daily bread. Forgive us our debts, as we also have forgiven our debtors. And lead us not into temptation, but deliver us from the evil one."

Matthew 6:9-13

Who Is on the Line?

When it comes time to pray, do you ever lose your focus or become easily distracted? Does it seem like your head becomes filled with many thoughts that interrupt your prayers? List ways you are easily distracted or situations that hinder you from prayer:

Distractions	Hindrances

When you pray, are you able to recognize God's voice? On many occasions the disciples witnessed Jesus spending time with His Father in prayer. There was something noticeably different and they wanted to know what made His prayer time different from theirs. In Luke 11:1, the disciples asked Jesus to teach them to pray.

Hallowed—The word, "hallowed" means "to make holy" or "to be sanctified." Jesus was teaching the disciples they were to be holy because He is holy. You bear the name Christian. As a believer, the life you live reflects the Father. 🏃

Plugged In

Jesus pursued an intimate relationship with His Heavenly Father through time spent alone in prayer. He understood prayer is a two-way communication with God. Read Matthew 6:9-13.

I. Holy is His Name

Prayer has the power to change lives. When we pray, we enter into God's presence and He becomes the focus of our prayer. Jesus taught us to pray, *Our Father, in heaven,* **hallowed** *be your name.*

Dr. Ken Hemphill tells the following story:

> I remember my Dad walking me to the car to give me my "going off to college" lecture. His words were surprisingly brief. He said, "Son, I have only one piece of advice to give you. I want to remind you that you bear my name. Your great-grandfather was a church planter and preacher; your grandfather was a godly man, and I think you know I've tried to live faithfully before God. The name Hemphill stands for something. So don't take my name anywhere I wouldn't take it, and don't involve my name in anything I wouldn't do." Although I didn't grasp at the time how important his advice would become, that reminder helped me many times through the years to make difficult but appropriate decisions when there was no one around to tell me what to do or how to behave. You see, our family reputation was at stake. Our name would be judged by the things I did and the places I went. I didn't have to worry so much about the specifics of splitting hairs or skirting the gray areas. I just had to see Dad's face in my mind, and I always knew without a doubt what I was supposed to do. In the same way, you and I bear the name of our heavenly Father. Therefore, everywhere we go and everything we do casts a reflection on Him.[1]

What did I do this week to hallow His name?
At school…
At work…
At home…
On a date…
At church…
With my friends…

II. Pray in Agreement

Jesus continued by saying, *Your kingdom come, your will be done on earth as it is in heaven.* Prayer adjusts you to God and enables you to know what He desires to do in and through your life. You are not making God's will adapt to your wants but releasing His will in you. The desire of your heart should be His Lordship over your life. As you pray, meditate on how you can be an active part of His kingdom's work.

III. Pray for Physical Needs

Read Matthew 6:26-31 and see how God takes care of everything we need. Make a list of physical needs these verses mention.

Jesus went on to teach, *Give us today our daily bread.* Pray to God on behalf of a physical need that exists in your life. God's provision makes you prepared for each day. He knows what you need. 🐾

Debts—The word Jesus used for "debts" (*opheilema* in the Greek) is another word for something owed or something due. It can be translated "fault" and carries with it the idea of conscious and deliberate transgression. We owe God our absolute obedience. When we are disobedient we can expect payment due. Jesus is calling us to admit our deliberate disobedience to God and ask for forgiveness.

IV. Pray Receiving Forgivenenss

Is there a little distance between you and God right now? Could it be unconfessed sin has wedged itself between you and Him? Write your name and "God" on a sheet of paper. Then, write any sins you are aware of in your life in a space between your name and God's.

Agree with God about that sin and confess it to Him. Think for a moment. What if God forgives you in the same way you have forgiven those who wrong you? You should not expect from God what you are not willing to give to others. God wants to purify you and make you clean. He desires to have a close relationship with you. Conclude your prayer by reading, *Forgive us our **debts**, as we also have forgiven our debtors.*

V. Pray for Protection

Jesus said, *And lead us not into temptation, but deliver us from the evil one.*
If you serve the Lord you are going to be tested and experience temptation.
Read 1 Corinthians 10:13 and Psalm 18:17-18. What do these verses say to
you? Are you facing any troubles or temptations? Take it to the Lord in prayer.

Through the Lord's Prayer, Jesus sought to lead the disciples to an understanding of prayer. The first part of the prayer focused on relating to God
and His honor and the last part to the needs of the person praying.

Scripture Speaks

Read the Scripture verses listed below and identify the elements of the Lord's
Prayer to which they relate. *(Check your answers at the end of the session.)*

_____ a. Matthew 18:19-20	I. Our Father in heaven, hallowed be your name.
_____ b. Psalm 103:12	
_____ c. Matthew 5:23-24	
_____ d. 1 John 5:14-15	II. Your kingdom come, your will be done on earth as it is in heaven.
_____ e. 2 Chronicles 7:14	
_____ f. Mark 11:24	
_____ g. Isaiah 12:4	III. Give us today our daily bread.
_____ h. Psalm 51:1-2	
_____ i. Psalm 139:23-24	IV. Forgive us our debts, as we also have forgiven our debtors.
_____ j. Proverbs 28:13	
_____ k. Psalm 46:10	
_____ l. 1 John 4:4	V. And lead us not into temptation but deliver us from the evil one.

Defined by Prayer

Are you a person of prayer? When the disciples witnessed Jesus after His
times in prayer they saw a difference in His life. He had a single focus and
was empowered to do the will of God. He had an intimate relationship with
His Heavenly Father. He called Him "Abba" meaning "daddy." Jesus modeled

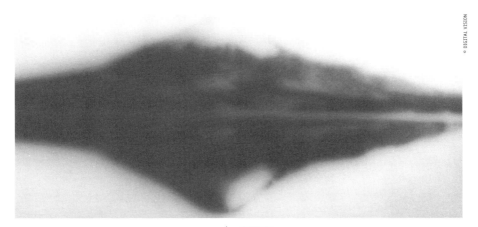

a life that was always plugged into His power source. When you cut off your communication with God, you are powerless. In the space below, write a poem or a letter depicting how your life has been changed through the power of God that comes through prayer.

1. Ken Hemphill, *The Prayer of Jesus*, pp. 47-48.

Answers for page 74 are I: g,k; II: a,e; III: d,f; IV: b,c,h,j; V: i,l..

BEYOND THE BASICS!

- Memorize Matthew 6:9-13 (The Lord's Prayer).
- Select a prayer partner and commit to praying with him or her once a week.
- Read the book *The Prayer of Jesus* by Ken Hemphill.
- Identify people whom you consider to be "prayer warriors." Interview two or three of them by asking, "How has prayer changed your lives?" and "How do you pray?"
- This week as you pray, expect God to answer. Be prepared to make adjustments in what He wants to do in your life.
- Motivate yourself to move from prayers that are general, "God bless all the missionaries," to more specific prayers, "God strengthen the Gaskin family today as they serve in Japan." Specific prayers better enable you to recognize when God answers.

© DIGITAL VISION

11. Calming the Storm

 Mark 4:35-41

MEMORY VERSE

Do not be anxious about anything, but in everything, by prayer and petition, with thanksgiving, present your requests to God. And the peace of God, which transcends all understanding, will guard your hearts and your minds in Christ Jesus.

Philippians 4:6-7

When the Storm Comes

In the fall of 1991, a fishing vessel called the *Andrea Gail* set out to sea from a port in Gloucester, MA. The crew went out looking for a good catch of fish but encountered more than they had bargained for. While on their way home, they were hit by what has come to be known as the "perfect storm." The storm that hit them was among the most powerful in recorded history and came about as a result of the collision of three hurricanes under the "perfect" conditions. They were simply in the wrong place at the very wrong time.[1]

Have you ever had one of those days, weeks, or even months when you felt like you were just in the wrong place at the wrong time? Life is going well, or so it seems, and then you are suddenly hit by a storm of proportions you didn't even know existed. The Bible promises we will have trouble in this life (John 16:33). Life will not always be smooth sailing.

You may even be in the middle of one of life's storms right now. If so, use the space below to describe the problem you are facing. If not, use this space to describe a storm you have faced in the past.

The Problem in Perspective

In Mark 4:35-41 the disciples were in a serious storm. Examining their response to the storm, as well as the response of Jesus, will help you find ways to deal with storms in your own life. Read the passage. Below, write some thoughts comparing the reactions of Jesus and the disciples to the storm.

Jesus

Disciples

The Sea of Galilee—A number of high mountains surround the Sea of Galilee. Often winds rush down the mountains and create sudden violent storms on the sea. Generally, the evening winds are the strongest winds of the day. Mark indicated Jesus and His disciples began their trip in the evening. Certainly, the disciples understood the gravity of their situation. As experienced fishermen, it is likely the disciples had encountered violent storms on the Sea of Galilee before. Yet, this storm caused these experienced seamen great anxiety. The men realized that if the boat continued to take on water, it would sink.

Quiet! Be Still!—The words Jesus used in Mark 4:39 were used in Mark 1:25 with reference to casting out a demon. The latter word in Greek, *pephimoso*, can be translated "be muzzled." Jesus, the God of nature, ordered the storm to shut its mouth. The fact that the waves died down immediately is significant. The immediate response of the waves demonstrates this was no coincidence. In the Old Testament, only God had the authority to control the forces of nature.

The biggest difference between how Jesus viewed the storm and how the disciples viewed it is a difference of perspective. The disciples focused only on the storm itself, while Jesus focused on the One who has power over all the storms. 🌞 This is an important point for us to remember. Often fear is born out of uncertainty. The disciples and Jesus had a different reality that night.

When we encounter difficult times in life, we are basically faced with two options. We can dwell on the uncertainty of our circumstances and drive ourselves crazy worrying about it, or we can trust God to bring us through it. We are so much better off when we trust God because He is able to see what lies ahead. He knows how and when the storm will end. We do not. On the scale below, circle the amount of trust you normally place in God when times get rough. A "1" means you are not willing to trust God at all and would rather weather the storm on your own. A "10" means you have complete trust in God no matter what life may bring.

| 1 | 2 | 3 | 4 | 5 | 6 | 7 | 8 | 9 | 10 |

Desperate, the disciples went to Jesus and awakened Him. They confronted Him with a pointed question: "Teacher, do you not care that we are perishing?" The disciples' tone seems accusatory. They are questioning whether or not Jesus cared about their fates. Though the disciples respond poorly in this situation, they obviously recognized Jesus possessed abilities they did not have. Otherwise, these fishermen would not have looked to a carpenter to save their lives. ⊤

God's Power on Display

You may be wondering why you should trust God to bring you through difficult situations. You may have questions about how He might accomplish this. The most important reason is He has the power to do for you what you cannot do for yourself. He often exercises that power in ways and timing you won't understand. Look at the passage again. The disciples were completely helpless in the midst of the storm, and they were afraid for their lives. Likely they had done all they knew how to do as experienced fishermen to handle the situation, which was beyond their control. They were overwhelmed by their circumstances and saw no possible method of relief. Jesus, on the other hand, was asleep and in complete peace. He simply got up and told the wind and waves to "**hush**." Do you know anyone who is able to control the weather? Meteorologists try to predict the weather, but they have no ability to control it. What we have in this passage is a display of the power of God in Jesus. That same power is available to help us when we trust Him with the difficulties we face. <GOD>

Are there areas in your life where you feel like you must have control? Oftentimes those are the areas to which God sends storms to teach us trust. List those areas below and ask God to help you turn those over to Him.

It's All About Faith

The reason we have so much fear and worry over the difficulties of life is that we do not have enough faith in God. In Joshua 1, the Lord gives us the promise that He will never leave or forsake us. Built into that promise is the fact that we do not have to fear because His power is always available to us. Therefore, the only real hindrance is our faith. Faith is the key to unlocking the power of God in our lives. Does that mean we will no longer face storms once we have faith? No, but it does mean we will be better prepared to make it through the storms. In the space below, write out a prayer asking God to help you to trust Him in the storm you are facing now or in ones you will face in the future.

BEYOND THE BASICS!

- Memorize Philippians 4:6-7.
- If you are currently in a difficult situation, try keeping a storm journal where each day you write about ways God is helping you deal with the problem. Be sure to praise Him for His power at work in bringing an end to your storm and for the things He teaches you through it.
- Interview someone in your church who has endured a great deal of difficulty and has a very strong faith in God. Ask the person how faith has impacted the way he or she has faced difficulties. See if the interview can be published in your youth newsletter or a church newsletter as an encouragement to others in your congregation.

---

1. Sources: *The Perfect Storm* by Sebastian Junger and www.perfectstorm.org.

12. Hungry?

Luke 9:10-17

© IMAGE STATE

MEMORY VERSE

Then Jesus declared, "I am the bread of life.
He who comes to me will never go hungry, and
he who believes in me will never be thirsty."

John 6:35

Fast Food Frenzy

Imagine the scene. You missed breakfast because you woke up late, and you skipped lunch so you could finish some homework due in one of your afternoon classes. After a hard day at school, you head to McDonald's® for a cheeseburger and fries. Needless to say, at this point in the day, you feel like you are starving to death. You enter the restaurant and nobody is waiting in line. Good news, considering the growling in your stomach. In fact, there is not another customer in the restaurant. At least you will get to enjoy your junk food in peace. You step up to the counter and utter those words that bring such joy to your own ears, "I'll have a number two, please." To your surprise, the response you get is not at all what you expected. "I'm sorry, but we're all out." Disappointed, you look briefly at the menu again and say, "O.K., then I'll have a number five please." This time, the response is one you never expected to hear. "Sorry, I must not have been clear the first time. We are all out of food today."

Circle your next response below.

1. "You have got to be kidding me. Am I on *Candid Camera* or something?"

2. "Yeah right, and I'm out of homework assignments."

3. "Well, then could you tell me where the nearest Burger King® is?"

4. "Ronald will be very disappointed when he hears about this."

5. "Uh, alright. Do you have any napkins I can chew on?"

For some, this may just seem like a silly situation. For others, it may be more like a nightmare. However you see it, the situation seems ridiculous because McDonald's never runs out of food. They may run out of mustard now and then, but they are never out of every item on the menu. The truth is we have grown accustomed to being able to walk into the nearest fast food joint and immediately satisfy our hunger. It is a part of life in America we take for granted. But what if we faced a real life situation when there really wasn't enough food?

Fantasy Becomes Reality

The disciples faced just such a situation. Not only that, but they faced it along with a hungry crowd of over 10,000 people. Read Luke 9:10-17. Verses 12-14 indicate the disciples faced what appeared to be an impossible situation. It was time for dinner, and they were out in a remote area with no McDonald's nearby. With them was a crowd of about 5,000 men plus women and children, which most likely totaled over 10,000 people. All they were able to scrounge up was five loaves of bread and two fish.

What do you think was the most likely outcome to this situation in the minds of the disciples?

1. Simon Peter would eat what little food there was before anyone else could get some.

2. They would be trampled alive by a hungry crowd of 10,000 people.

3. Jesus would make His own gourmet meal out of a rock and some twigs and they would be left with Long John Silvers® value meals.

4. The crowd would perish of starvation before Pizza Hut® could deliver.

What would you have done if you had been one of the disciples? Write your answer in the space provided.

And God Steps In

Jesus did what the disciples thought was impossible. He took the food they had gathered and fed all 10,000 people as much as they could eat. He even managed to leave a doggy bag for each of the disciples. Jesus took the food the disciples saw as "next to nothing" and turned it into an all-you-can-eat buffet! This miracle teaches us about the greatness of God and about how much He loves us and desires to provide for us. 🔆 Take a moment to look at the list below and mark out any of the items on the list not ultimately provided for us by God.

Life	**Breath**
Heartbeat	**Clothing**
Food	**Home**
Family	**Health**
Church	**Bible**
Brain	**Love**

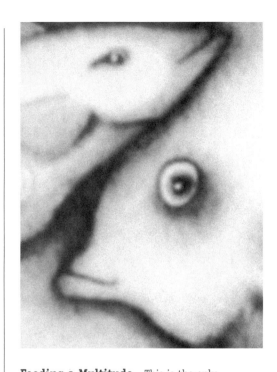

Feeding a Multitude—This is the only recorded miracle of Jesus recorded in all four Gospels. Each Gospel has the same basic information but from slightly different perspectives. At this point in Jesus' life, His ministry was becoming quite well known. The preceding chapters in Luke described large crowds following Him. His teaching captivated audiences, and the news of His healing ministry offered hope to those in need. This particular teaching event took place in a desolate area outside the city of Bethsaida. It was more like a remote area outside of town than a barren desert. Bethsaida was a small village located on the northeast side of the Sea of Galilee. Its name means "house of fish" and it was the home of Andrew, Peter and Philip.

Do the Math—Take a few minutes and figure out how much money it would take to physically feed the crowd of 10,000 in happy meals. Figure a happy meal at $2.50. A denarius was equal to a day's wage or about $40. Fill in the math below for the amounts. Note: Obviously, their expense for meals was less than today's happy meal since Mark and John indicated 8 months wages would not be enough to buy food for the crowd. That would be about 210 denarii.

10,000 People

x $2.50 (Happy Meal Cost)

_____

= $_____ /$40 (A Day's Wage)

= _____ Denarii.

Hopefully, you were not able to mark out any of the items on the list. The truth is, our loving Heavenly Father provides for our basic needs. Never take for granted the graces that surround us everyday, all day.

Unusual Circumstances

The disciples had just returned from their ministry journey. Before Jesus sent them off, He commanded: "Take nothing for the journey—no staff, no bag, no bread, no money, no extra tunic" (Luke 9:3). The lesson to be learned in this life moment was dependence. They needed to trust in God to provide. When you first glance at the reactions of Christ's disciples in the feeding of the 5,000, you may be prompted to think it was a lesson poorly learned. However, don't discount the fact they did bring what little they had to Jesus. John indicates that it was Andrew who brought the five loaves and two fish to Jesus. Perhaps it was out of curiosity; perhaps it was an act of dumb obedience. Nevertheless, they made their meager resources available to Christ. At the very least, we should be like the disciples here and bring whatever we have to Christ.

When everyone was seated, Jesus took the bread and the fish and He looked to heaven and blessed the food. This action demonstrated Jesus' dependence upon the Father. We should note Jesus' inclusion of the disciples in the performance of this miracle. He used this miracle as an opportunity to show them He is the ultimate source of provision.

▼ The disciples likely considered a number of sources that might offer provision for the crowd. Yet, Jesus met the needs of the crowd with an abundance of food remaining. Jesus wants His followers to recognize His ability to meet any need. Finally, we should not allow the availability (or unavailability) of physical resources to create boundaries in ministry. The power of Christ is not limited to things that are visible.

In the space below write a thank you note to God for supplying all of your needs.

 BEYOND THE BASICS!

- Memorize John 6:35.
- If your church has a food pantry or clothes closet for the needy, offer your services there as a personal ministry project.
- Commit to praying before every meal and thanking God for your food. This is not only a great way to remember God's provision, but it can also be a powerful witness to those who do not know God.
- Fasting is a great way to learn to appreciate all God provides for us and to grow in your relationship with Him. Fasting is a forgotten and neglected spiritual discipline, even though Jesus talked a great deal about it. (For example, see Matthew 6:16-18.) Commit to fasting as a part of your spiritual growth, but before doing so read chapter four in Richard Foster's book entitled *Celebration of Discipline* which deals with how to fast.

Dear God,

13. Power Over Life and Death

 John 11:17-46

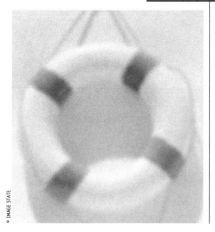

MEMORY VERSE

Jesus said to her, "I am the resurrection and the life. He who believes in me will live, even though he dies."

John 11:25

Where Is God?

Have you ever tried to imagine how you would feel if you lost someone close to you? Christian author C.S. Lewis is best known for his children's books, *The Chronicles of Narnia.* However, when his wife died, his writing became much more stark and painful. The following is from his book, *A Grief Observed.*

> No one ever told me that grief felt so like fear. I am not afraid, but the sensation is like being afraid. The same fluttering in the stomach, the same restlessness, the yawning. I keep on swallowing.

> At other times it feels like being mildly drunk, or concussed. There is a sort of invisible blanket between the world and me. I find it hard to take in what anyone says. Or perhaps, hard to want to take in what anyone says. It is so uninteresting. Yet I want the others to be about me. I dread the moments when the house is empty. If only they would talk to one another and not to me.

And no one ever told me about the laziness of grief. Except at my job—where the machine seems to run on much as usual—I loathe the slightest effort. Not only writing but even reading a letter is too much. Even shaving. What does it matter now whether my cheek is rough or smooth? They say an unhappy man wants distractions—something to take him out of himself. Only as a dog-tired man wants an extra blanket on a cold night; he'd rather lie there shivering than get up and find one. It's easy to see why the lonely become untidy, finally, dirty and disgusting.

Meanwhile, where is God?[1]

The question "Where is God?" has been asked by countless people who have encountered true grief. It is a question most people ask at some time in their lives. God is not too small to answer it, nor is He so big that He overlooks our pain. Grief brings a sense of loneliness along with many other emotions. So, how does a Christian deal with grief? Before going on, underline three words or phrases from the excerpt above that stand out to you. Explain why you chose those particular words or phrases in the space below.

Denial

Shock

Anger

Bargaining

Guilt

Depression

Loneliness

Acceptance

Hope

Crying

Laughing

Singing

Playing

Sleeping

Eating

Frowning

Smiling

Hugging

Change

Reading

Defining Grief

Write a definition of the word "grief" in your own words.

Grief is associated with many different feelings and actions. Circle the words in the list at the left that you would most commonly associate with grief.

In reality, everything listed can be associated with grief. The first thing we must know about grief is that it is a process—not an event. Grief can take many forms, and it always takes time.

Character Comparison

Now let's look at a Scripture passage where Jesus dealt with grief. Read John 11:17-37. Notice the different ways Mary, Martha, and Jesus expressed the emotional pain they were feeling. List what you observed about each character in the space at the top of the next page.

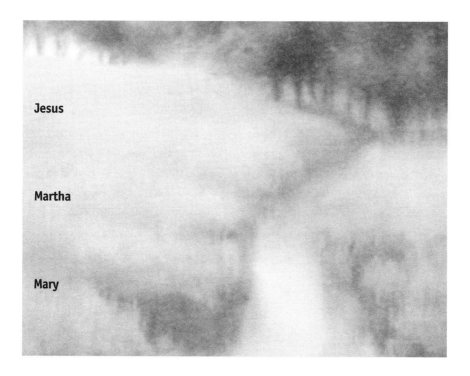

Jesus

Martha

Mary

You should have recognized both similarities and differences in the way the two sisters dealt with their grief. Martha chose to take action and not to wait for something to happen. This is why she ran to meet Jesus as soon as she heard He was in town. On the other hand, Mary chose to stay home until Jesus called for her. Mary was content to wait; she didn't feel like she had to act immediately.

The grief process can look very different from person to person. Some like to stay busy while others prefer to lie around. Some like to talk while others prefer to be left alone. One way is not better than another; they are simply different. Both sisters reveal different ways of dealing with the loss of a loved one.

There is one striking similarity in the way the sisters approached Jesus. They both approached Him with the same words. (Compare verses 21 and 32.) They both made statements that began with "if." If we are honest, we have made similar statements ourselves. These statements are the result of uncertain moments. Review the final words of the excerpt you read earlier. One of the questions we face in times of grief is, where is God when I am hurting?

I am—The passage records one of the most powerful "I am" statements in the Gospel of John. Jesus said, "I am the resurrection and the life." The writer used two powerful images that pictured Jesus as the giver and sustainer of life. Jesus is our strength in life; He is present at every stage of our lives. The word used for "life" in this passage isn't simply referring to our physical lives. It refers to our entire being—both physical and spiritual. ▼

 BEYOND THE BASICS!

- Memorize John 11:25.
- Read *A Grief Observed* by C.S. Lewis. (It is only about twenty pages long.)
- Send a sympathy card to a friend or classmate who has recently lost a loved one.
- Volunteer at a local nursing home. Helping others can be a rewarding learning experience. Many nursing homes also have an "Adopt a Grandparent" program in which you can participate.
- Make plans to visit a funeral home or set up an appointment to talk with your pastor. Ask the funeral home staff or your pastor how they minister to grieving people.

The Presence of Christ

Not only is Christ present with us but He also joins us in our grief. Hebrews 4:14-16 clearly states Jesus was tempted just as we are. He became tired just as we do. He suffered just as we do. Jesus knows what we face. And He goes through it with us—just as He did with Mary and Martha. ▼

The Power of Christ

You can trust Christ in the midst of grief because He has power over life and death. Read John 11:38-46. Jesus showed us what will take place with everyone who places their faith in Him. Death is by no means the end. Because of what Christ has done in the life of every believer, we have no reason to fear death and we have every reason to live in complete response to our faith in Jesus. He has given us an amazing promise through His sacrifice. In the space below, write a prayer to God praising Him for removing the power of death and the fear it causes through the awesome gift of life—eternal life—that we have in Jesus.

---

1. Lewis, C.S., *A Grief Observed*. New York: Seabury Press, 1963.

Rooted or Rootless?

 Mark 4:3-20

MEMORY VERSE

"Others, like seed sown on good soil, hear the word, accept it, and produce a crop—thirty, sixty or even a hundred times what was sown."

Mark 4:20

Telling Stories

Since the beginning of civilization, cultures have used storytelling to translate information from one generation to the next. The culture's morals, ideals, heritage, and even political rules were passed down in the form of stories. The Hebrew tribes of the Old Testament, the Sub-Saharan African nations, Native American groups in our own country, and current day Aboriginal people of Australia have all included storytelling as a means of cultural survival. Researchers call this an oral tradition, and in many parts of the world, it is still an important means of developing cultural identity.

Oral tradition is a main part of how we know about Jesus and His teachings. Think about the turmoil that surrounded Jesus and His disciples! Crowds of people followed them everywhere, the Jewish rulers plotted against Jesus, fear and doubt surrounded His Crucifixion, and wonder and hope swelled in His resurrection. Can't you just see the disciples sitting around a table comparing stories, talking about what Jesus had done when He was with them, and telling the amazing story of His death and resurrection? The Gospels (Matthew,

Mark, Luke, and John) are God-inspired stories about Jesus. Sharing stories is an important element in the process that gave us the Bible as we know it.

Jesus used storytelling throughout His ministry. Called **parables**, His stories helped explain truths about the Kingdom of God and the hope that is in Christ. They taught people how to live as Christians, how to act towards their neighbors and enemies alike, and how to be a meaningful influence in their community. These stories help us understand difficult concepts and teach us what it means to be followers of Christ.

Telling Parables

Before we look at one of Jesus' parables, there are two things to keep in mind:

- They can be understood on two levels—physical and spiritual. The spiritual level becomes easier to understand when we identify the physical level first.

- The key to understanding a parable is knowing what role you play in the parable being told.

Parable—The word "parable" comes from the Greek verb *paraballein* that means, "to throw beside." Jesus told stories about things people of that day were familiar with. He told stories about working in the fields, weddings, and banquets. However, his parables had a heavenly meaning "thrown beside" the earthly meaning.

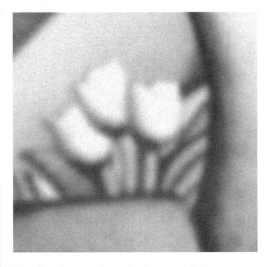

Teach—The Greek verb "to teach" in Mark 4:2 is *didasko*. Teaching traditionally happened in the synagogue. Jesus was doing something new; He was teaching in the open air. He was teaching in public, where the people were. If this was not radical enough, Jesus was using a radical new method. He was teaching in parables. The teaching of Jesus was powerful (Mark 1:22). In fact, when people addressed Jesus in the Gospels, they most often called Him "Teacher."

Rootless?

What does it take for a seed to grow into a plant? What does it take for a seed to live and not die? Using the list below, identify the necessary ingredients for a seed to grow into a plant.

❑ **Rich soil**　　❑ **Cultivated soil**　　❑ **Water**　　❑ **Fertilizer**

❑ **Sunshine**　　❑ **Shade**　　　　❑ **Cold weather**　　❑ **Attention**

All of these, to some extent, are necessary ingredients for growth. Some seeds require shade while others require complete sun to develop fully. There are certain conditions necessary for any seed to experience growth.

Mark records Jesus' **teaching** about the Parable of the Seeds and what is required for the seeds to grow.

Read Mark 4:3-9. Complete the chart below to determine the differences between the situations described.

Specific Verses	Type of Soil	Environment Around the Soil	What Happened to the Seed
Mark 4:4			
Mark 4:5-6			
Mark 4:7			
Mark 4:8			

Circle the examples of soil where the seed was unable to develop strong roots. Why are strong roots important?

Rooted?

Remember that a parable has two levels—physical and spiritual. The previous chart helps identify the physical. Read Mark 4:9 again. Jesus knew only those who had spiritual discernment would be able to understand the spiritual message of the parable. Jesus went on to explain the spiritual meaning of the types of soil for the disciples.

Read Mark 4:10-20. Use the same process used above to identify the spiritual message of this parable. Complete the chart below to compare the physical details of this parable with Jesus' explanation.

Hear, Accept, Produce—Verse 8 contains a succession of present tense verbs. This tense suggests continuous, ongoing action. When the writer writes "hear the word, accept it, and produce a crop" it is the same as if he would have written "hearing the word, accepting it, and producing a crop." In other words, the seed is active and engaged in growth. Our lives should consistently plunge into the depths of God's Word and become more rooted in Christ.

Specific Verses	Physical Soil	Spiritual Soil	What Happens
Mark 4:15			
Mark 4:16-17			
Mark 4:18-19			
Mark 4:20			

Review your responses to determine which of the examples above demonstrates a spiritual life rooted in God's Word.

I realize that my spiritual life

is like

_____

(type of spiritual soil).
Because of that,
I am becoming
(more/less)
like Christ.

BEYOND THE BASICS!

- Memorize Mark 4:20.
- Write the story of your relationship with Jesus. Find an opportunity this week to share your story with a friend.
- Develop a plan to prepare the soil of your heart to better receive the seed of God's Word. Write your plan in your journal. Include specific actions.

Are You Rooted?

What creates good spiritual soil? If a seed needs sunlight, water, and nourishment to survive, what does faith need to grow and develop? Circle those things listed below that can keep the soil of your heart fertile for God's Word to grow:

–Time in prayer

–Time in Bible study

–Time developing Christian mentors

–Time sharing your faith

–Time searching for God's will

 in your life

What other actions would you add to the list above?

Look at what you circled. How fertile is the soil of your heart for God's Word? Do the roots of God's Word go deep or shallow into the soil of your heart? Fill in the sentence at the top left of the page.

Is this an accurate description of your life? How will you allow God's Word to become firmly rooted in you?

15. Why Forgive?

 Matthew 18:21-35

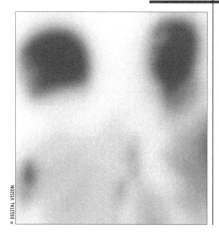

MEMORY VERSE

Bear with each other and forgive whatever grievances you may have against one another. Forgive as the Lord forgave you.

Colossians 3:13

© DIGITAL VISION

Forgiving Is Hard!

Atlanta Thrashers' Dany Heatley has learned how hard it is to forgive. He's had to learn not only to forgive himself but also to accept the forgiveness of others.

Dany was returning home with his friend and fellow teammate, Dan Snyder, late one evening. While driving his Ferrari well over the posted speed limit, Dany lost control of his car. In the resulting crash, the car was torn in half and totally demolished. Dany suffered injuries to his jaw. Dan Snyder, however, was critically injured with a depressed skull fracture. He never regained consciousness and lived only six days after the accident.

Dany was understandably devastated. His best friend had died, and he had been driving. When he spoke publicly for the first time about the accident, he was overcome with grief for his friend. Dan's family had every right to be bitter and angry about his death. Instead, they chose to forgive Dany. At Dan's funeral, his father said, "We want you to know we do not lay blame on Dany Heatley for the accident that took our son from us. Forgiveness is also a part of being human and we are here to support him through this difficult time." It was the support and the forgiveness of the Snyder family that helped Dany work through this time.

Dany returned to the ice with the Thrashers almost four months to the day after the car crash. He wore Dan's number 37 on a patch over his heart—a sign Dan had not been forgotten.

Forgiveness is hard, both to give and to receive. In the Parable of the Unmerciful Servant, Jesus examined how someone could accept forgiveness from one person and yet not give the same level of forgiveness to another.

What Is Forgiveness?

In the space provided, write your best definition for forgiveness.

© IMAGE 100

The Psychology of Forgiveness—In an effort to understand the health differences between believers and nonbelievers, scientists are beginning to analyze the individual aspects of religious experiences. Using brain scans, researchers have discovered that . . . intangibles, such as the impact of forgiveness, may boost health as well. A survey of 1,500 people found that people who forgive easily tend to enjoy greater psychological well-being and have less depression than those who hold grudges. "There's a physiology of forgiveness," said Dr. Herbert Benson, head of the Mind/Body Medical Institute. "When you do not forgive, it will chew you up."[1]

To forgive is to give up resentment against or the desire to punish; to stop being angry with; to cancel a debt.

What makes forgiveness hard for you? List below the feelings you have that make forgiveness hard to give and to receive:

Can You Limit Forgiveness?

Jesus constantly challenged the teaching of the religious authorities. In Matthew 18:21-35, He used a parable to question their teachings once again. One area of Jewish teaching was forgiveness. Jewish custom required a Jew to forgive a brother or sister three times. However, on the fourth time, the Jew was under no obligation to forgive the sin. In this passage, Peter asked Jesus how often he should forgive someone. He even suggested a number more than twice the Jewish standard—seven. Read Matthew 18:21-22.

Jesus' response went far beyond Peter's question or expectations. Peter thought he was being generous using the number seven. Likely, he was completely blown away by what Jesus suggested. How many times did Jesus tell Peter to forgive someone?

Did you start multiplying numbers together? Actually, Jesus didn't use the number to identify a precise amount, but to illustrate a general attitude towards forgiveness. Jesus' teaching was that we should always forgive.

What Happens When You Don't Forgive?

Jesus understood this was a difficult concept to grasp, so He used a parable to explain it. The parable is about three men and how they handled collecting a debt owed them. Read Matthew 18:23-34 and identify the two opportunities for forgiveness. On the next page list the verse in which the opportunity was presented, who was present, and whether forgiveness was given:

1.

2.

Did you notice when the servant asked the king for forgiveness, he forgave the entire debt? Some translations say the servant owed ten thousand talents. A talent was the largest denomination of money the Greeks had, and the number ten thousand was the highest number for which there was a Greek word. That would be an unbelievable amount of money. Yet the king forgave the debt. 🏃🏃

You would think the forgiveness given to the servant would have changed him forever. But it didn't. He left the king, found a servant who owed him a hundred denarii, or about three to four thousand dollars, and demanded his money. When he didn't get what he was owed, he had the servant thrown in jail until he could pay in full. The man who had been forgiven a huge debt did not forgive a much smaller one.

Denarius=One day's wage (approximately $30-$40)

Talent=Approximately 5,000 denarii

10,000 Talents=Approximately 50 million denarii (somewhere around two trillion dollars)

Herod's annual salary was 900 talents

The tax for Galilee and Perea together was only 200 talents

His unforgiving spirit caused him to lose the forgiveness he had been given by the king. The unforgiving servant was sent to prison until he too could pay his debt in full. He would be in prison forever!

A Debt I Could Not Pay

There is a huge difference between the two debts mentioned in this parable. The first was a debt that even a king could not repay in a lifetime while the other debt amounted to less than six months' of work wages. Ironically, it is the lesser of the two amounts that the unmerciful servant—who had just been

Verse 35 is written in such a way as to suggest potential action or what might happen to someone who acts like the unmerciful servant. Within this one verse, the potential action is contained within a conditional (i.e. If/then) statement. This verse is not proof of an angry God. Rather, the writer of this text simply explained that those who are unable to forgive others have not genuinely experienced the forgiveness of God through the sacrifice of His Son. And those who have not accepted the forgiveness available through Jesus have not received the mercy of the Master.

 ## BEYOND THE BASICS!

- Memorize Colossians 3:13.
- Study Luke 23:32-43 to discover how Jesus demonstrated forgiveness when even He was suffering the most.
- Identify one individual you look up to that is a great example of someone who demonstrates forgiveness. Schedule a time to talk with the person about where he or she first learned about forgiveness, how it has impacted his or her life, and how he or she practices forgiveness daily.

forgiven of the much greater debt— enforced. God paid for our sin through the death of Jesus on the cross—a debt we can never repay. He has made forgiveness available to all humanity. His action for us was so selfless it is overwhelming.

Read Matthew 18:35. The end of the parable reminds us we must forgive because we are forgiven. Forgiving is not easy. People hurt us; they make us angry. It can be difficult to let go of that anger and hurt. Yet, God forgave us. We must also learn to forgive. ▼

On a separate sheet of paper, write all the sins you can remember, no matter how big or small. After you have exhausted your memory, read the list. Ask God to forgive you and then destroy it completely. When you have completed this activity, write all the sins committed against you or that hurt you along with the name of the offender. After you have exhausted your memory, read this list. Ask God to help you forgive those on the list and then destroy it completely.

---

1. Claudia Kalb, "Faith and Healing," *Newsweek*, Nov 3, 2003: http://msnbc.msn.com/id/3403642

16. Lost and Found

Luke 15:11-32

© RUBBERBALL PRODUCTIONS

MEMORY VERSE

For the Son of Man came to seek and to save what was lost.

Luke 19:10

Being Lost

Dr. Beck Weathers constantly pushed himself; he was always ready for the next challenge. Unfortunately, his next challenge almost killed him. In 1996, he was caught in the worst storm in history on Mt. Everest. Dr. Weathers, along with a team of five climbers and their professional guide, made their summit attempt during the night. However, the storm hit before most of the team could make it back down the mountain to safety. The guide, Rob Hall, died trying to save the team. Five team members and eight climbers died. Dr. Weathers himself was twice left for dead, once only 300 yards from his camp. He survived but lost his nose, right hand, and part of his left hand to the frostbite he suffered. When Dr. Weathers wandered into camp the next morning, he was a frightening sight. His teammates had given him up for dead twice, but they rejoiced that he was alive.[1]

Jesus emphasized that God places value on every human being because we are all important to Him. Jesus spent time with people who were sinners. As a result, the Pharisees and other religious leaders complained that He associated with people who were unworthy. Jesus told three parables to emphasize how important it is to an owner to find what they have lost.

Lost Things

On a scale of 1-10, rank each of the following on what causes you stress when you lose it, 10 being the most stressful.

___ Keys	___ Identification	___ Wallet
___ Dog	___ Homework	___ Sibling
___ Sports Game	___ Bible	___ Shoe
___ Jewelry	___ Boyfriend/Girlfriend	___ Weight
___ Hair	___ Music CD	___ Game Piece
___ Article of Clothing	___ Your Way	___ Book
___ Collectible	___ Cell Phone	___ Calendar/PDA

Two of the three parables are relatively short; the third is much longer. In the first parable (Luke 15:3-7), Jesus told of a shepherd who had one hundred sheep. When one sheep wandered away from the rest, the shepherd left the ninety-nine to find the one lost sheep. He reminded His listeners that just like the lost sheep and the shepherd, God will search for one lost sinner even when ninety-nine remain righteous. 👫

The second parable (Luke 15:8-10) is about a woman who had ten valuable coins. When she lost a coin, she cleaned her house until she found it. Once she found the coin, she called in her neighbors to celebrate. Jesus again reminded His listeners God will not give up His search. That coin was obviously very valuable to the woman who lost it. Just think how much more valuable you are to your Creator. 👫

Lost People

Jesus used all three parables to teach about the value God places on the lost world. The third parable is the most widely known of the three. It's also the most developed story. Following is a list of the key characters:

- **The Father**—very loving and allowed the sons to make their own choices
- **The Prodigal Son**—wanted his share of his inheritance so he could have his freedom
- **The Faithful Son**—stayed behind and resented his brother's choices

Of the two brothers in the story, which one do you identify with the most? Why?

The prodigal or lost son discovered that freedom was not all he expected it to be. Read Luke 15:14-19. What changes in his lifestyle did he choose to make as a result of his freedom? List these below:

The prodigal son had to realize his choices were destructive and his intentions were wrong before he would ask his father to take him

The Purpose of Christ—Just a few chapters over, Jesus clearly stated His purpose: "to save what was lost" (Luke 19:10). Each of these parables demonstrate what a person who has lost something is willing to do to find it. None of these three stories compare to what God has already done to rescue you. Jesus gave His life to give you a way home. You don't have to be lost forever.

Parables of Lost Things

back—even as a servant. Read Luke 15:20-32. His father had been anticipating his son's return because he recognized him from a long way off. His father not only welcomed him back but also fully restored him as his son.

What was the brother's reaction? Was his behavior justified? The one brother had stayed behind and his brother took half of their inheritance and wasted it. Was it fair for his brother to come back and be made a son of the house again? How would you have felt?

God is Waiting—When his father saw his son, the Bible says he was "filled with compassion." Don't you find that interesting? The father didn't say, "I told you so." He was thrilled to see his son home again. He knew exactly what had happened. God is also filled with compassion when we decide to return home. He isn't caught up in the reasons why we left or even why we have been gone so long. He put all that behind Him at the cross. God is waiting for you, and He, too, will recognize you from a distance and be filled with compassion. ▼

The brother who stayed home is often unnoticed because there is so much attention given to the son who left with his inheritance. If you have been faithful to God, it's easy to be upset with those who are not. You must guard against this attitude. Nobody deserves the mercy and grace God freely gives to all humanity. Have you been faithful to God? Do you feel like you deserve more than those who have not been faithful? If so, remember the price Jesus paid for even your smallest sins. All people are equal in God's eyes and deserve a way home.

Although it was hard for the brother who stayed behind, his brother was welcomed back completely—no strings attached. Jesus made it clear: No matter what you have done, who you are, or where you've been, God is waiting to welcome you home. Every person is valuable to God—not just those who are faithful but those who have been unfaithful too.

Lost World

God's love for us is stated plainly in John 3:16—"For God so loved the world that he gave his one and only son, that whoever believes in him will not perish but have eternal life." There is no question God cares about the entire world. What should your response be to those who are lost? How can you accurately present God's love to them?

1.*Into Thin Air*, John Krackauker., New York: Anchor Books, 1997.

BEYOND THE BASICS!

- Memorize Luke 15:10.
- Identify your friends who are likely lost. Begin to pray earnestly for them to find God's grace.
- Study Matthew 9:35-38 to determine what responsibility you have for caring for the lost.
- Complete a personal evangelism training course or read a book about personal evangelism and begin to practice sharing your faith with the lost friends you listed in the previous step.

© DIGITAL VISION

17. A **Second** Birthday

 John 3:1-21

MEMORY VERSE

For God so loved the world that he gave his one and only Son, that whoever believes in him shall not perish but have eternal life.

John 3:16

New Life

What person at some point in his or her life has not been amazed by butterflies? When we are young, we are fascinated by their colors and effortless flight. We are also curious about the strange-looking caterpillars but don't immediately make the connection between the larva and the winged insects. When we get a little older we begin to learn about the cocooning process and the chrysalis stage. During larva stage a caterpillar will increase 30,000 times its original size. The creatures are slow, eat hundreds of times their body weight, live anywhere from one month to three years in this stage, and never travel more than a few feet from where they were hatched. Silkworms will eat up to 10 pounds of mulberry leaves to manufacture 1 pound of cocoon, which can be spun into a silk thread 100 miles long.

During the chrysalis stage, their larva characteristics dissolve and the metamorphosis is completed within a cocoon that will usually last anywhere from one week to seven months. Once the transformation is complete, a beautiful butterfly emerges and can experience flight. Butterflies live from two to four weeks, but it can be an incredible lifespan. The Monarch butterflies migrate between Southern Canada and Central Mexico, a distance of about 2,500 miles. They weigh only 1/50 of an ounce but travel at speeds of 20 miles per hour and at altitudes as high as 10,000 feet.[1]

Metamorphosis is indeed a miraculous process. Believers can also experience a transformation as dramatic as the butterfly's. Jesus explained this re-birth process to a curious religious leader who was searching for answers.

The Transformation of Nicodemus

Nicodemus was a big shot in the Jewish community and a member of the Jewish equivalent of the Supreme Court. He had memorized all the rules of his faith. In addition, his money gave him power and position in his culture. Though he was a well-respected teacher and member of the largest religious group himself, Nicodemus apparently had great respect for Jesus. That's why he called Him "Rabbi." Though it was a title of honor, it didn't capture the complete person of Jesus. Jesus wanted Nicodemus to understand that everyone needed to be born again by God's Spirit. Only the Spirit of God can **breathe** life into our souls. Just like the wind, the Spirit cannot be seen or touched. The Holy Spirit reveals Jesus' identity and His work.

After reading John 3:1-8, match these key words or phrases to their explanations. (*Answers can be found at the end of this session.*)

_____ **1. Pharisees** (v. 1)

_____ **2. Rabbi** (v. 2)

_____ **3. Signs/miracles** (v. 2)

_____ **4. Born again** (vv. 3, 7)

_____ **5. second time** (v. 4)

_____ **6. kingdom of God** (v. 5)

_____ **7. spirit** (v. 6)

_____ **8. wind** (v. 8)

a. God's intervention to reveal Himself.

b. A spiritual second birth; also means "from above."

c. Repeated action.

d. Essence of being that cannot be seen or manipulated but is identified by the effects it brings.

e. A word that means "breath" and "spirit" in Greek as well.

f. The place where God's reign is complete.

g. Teacher.

h. Influential Jews who believed that keeping rules and staying away from sinners was the way to please God.

Breath—the Greek work often translated as "spirit" or "breath" is *pneuma*. It is similar to the Hebrew word *ruach*—the word used when God "breathed" life into Adam. The idea of spirit is much deeper than school spirit or pride. It refers to the eternal life force or the spiritual dimension of our being—the part of our being that truly makes us alive.

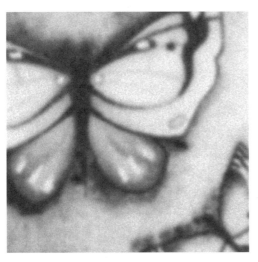

Born Again—*Genethe Anothen* is the Greek phrase found in verses 3 and 7 that is most commonly translated as "born again." The phrase literally means to be born from above. The passive voice of this verb suggests we are unable to do this ourselves; it must be done to us. This process begins and ends with Jesus. Believing in Him and accepting Him as our Lord and Savior is the only way to be born from above.

Comparisons

Nicodemus knew a lot of Scripture, but he didn't completely understand the impact God's power could have on a human life. Only God can give us a new heart and a spirit consistent with His mind and motives. Jesus was aware Nicodemus did not understand the foundational concept of new birth.

Jesus reminded Nicodemus of the story of Moses lifting the serpent to provide God's solution to the snakebites the children of Israel were enduring. In a similar way, Jesus was going to be lifted up on the cross to take away the sin of all humans—God's solution for humankind's sin. ▼

After reading John 3:9-15 explain these three key phrases:

• **earthly versus heavenly (v. 12)**

• **Son of Man and the serpent (vv. 13-14)**

• **eternal life versus eternal separation (v. 15).**

Answer these two questions:

Did Nicodemus know enough about God to get into heaven?

In what way was Christ lifted up?

Shining Brightly

John 3:16 comprises the good news of Jesus Christ in one simple verse. It describes God's plan to rescue us from our sin. He loved us so much He sent His only Son so we could believe in Him and never die.

God treasures us. He does not condemn us to the punishment we deserve. Instead, He provided a sacrifice for those sins. If we are condemned, then it is because we choose not to believe. The difference between a person who believes in God and one who does not is not measured in terms of guilt or innocence—since we are all guilty apart from Christ. The difference lies in the life of the individual. An unbelieving person wants to hide from God's light, which exposes sin. The believing person lives in response to the sacrifice Jesus made on the cross and the resurrection that took place three days later.

Read John 3:16-21. Circle the phrases printed below that represent light and put an "X" on the ones that represent darkness.

Chooses to be condemned.	**Came into the world.**
Men loved it more than goodness.	**Represents truth.**
Avoids the light.	**Truth-seekers are drawn to it.**
Represents evil deeds.	**Longs to have its deeds exposed plainly.**
Fears exposure of evil.	**Does not condemn.**
Hates light.	**Points to the salvation of the world.**

BEYOND THE BASICS!

- Memorize John 3:16.
- Choose one friend for whom you will rewrite Jesus' explanation of how to find Him without using any "churchy" words. You may want to mix this with your testimony.
- Read John 3:16 inserting *when* and the another person's name in place of *whosoever* or *whoever* as a means of praying for lost friends.
- Ask yourself: What things stop me from sharing about the new birth? What would it cost me to share about Christ more often?
- Celebrate your "second birthday" by throwing a party to commemorate the day you invited Jesus into your heart. Invite friends and a youth leader to lead in a special prayer to share Christ with your friends and to renew your commitment to follow Him.

Answers to page 107:
1h, 2g, 3a, 4b, 5c, 6f, 7d, and 8e.

Although God is unseen, a Christian is a witness for God people can see, hear, and touch. Are you living in the light or avoiding His presence? Reflect on that question, then write a prayer to God in the space below asking for His constant presence in your life.

1. Butterflies 2000:
wwwthebutterflysite.com/biology.shtml

Samaria at the Time of Christ

Note Mount Gerizim where the Samaritans had built a temple to worship God. Also note the possible site of Jacob's well.

18.I Gotta **Do What?**

 Luke 10:25-37

MEMORY VERSE

He answered: " 'Love the Lord your God with all your heart and with all your soul and with all your strength and with all your mind'; and, 'Love your neighbor as yourself.'"

Luke 10:27

Different Crowd

By high school, T.J. Ware had become known as his academy's ultimate troublemaker. He wasn't very talkative, got into fights, and had ignored his teachers to the point of flunking every class by the time he entered his senior year. One weekend the entire student body was given the opportunity to attend a leadership retreat. One of the main leaders of the school listened intently to the opening overview of the weekend: "We have a total spectrum represented today from the student body president to T.J. Ware, the boy with the longest arrest record in the history of town."

T.J. didn't participate initially, but he began to develop a change of heart when his small group listened and acknowledged his ideas. His group took the time to love him despite his track record of instigating problems. Although it was probably very difficult for the students to give him a chance, T.J. needed their love and attention. Surprisingly, he had incredible ideas for the Homeless Project team. Two weeks after the retreat, T.J. and his new friends organized a group of 70 students to collect food. They gathered 2,854 cans of food in just two hours, which was an amazing school record. There was enough food to stock shelves in two neighboring centers, which provided 75 days of meals for various families. T.J. began making an effort with school studies as well by showing up for all classes and finally participating. He initiated a second project that produced a collection of 300 blankets and 1,000 pairs of shoes for the area homeless shelter![1]

People are hurting all around us. Some of them live next door and others sit next to us in school. God calls for us to minister people in need. It doesn't matter how different from us they may be, they are in need of God's love. During Jesus' ministry, an individual wanted Jesus to qualify the kinds of people to whom they were to minister. Jesus used an extreme example of reaching across barriers to meet the needs of people.

Identify Them

Think of the students in your school that either do not have many friends or who remind you of T.J. Can you think of times when other people have treated them poorly? What were the situations and what was your response? Jot them below.

Situation	Your Response
Lee made fun of Troy's shoes.	I looked the other way and acted like I didn't notice.

Read Luke 10:25-37. A **lawyer** who knew Old Testament Scripture was testing Jesus by asking how to obtain eternal life. Jesus asked the lawyer what the Scriptures said. The lawyer quoted a part of the Scriptures called the "shema." It was a passage well known to all Jews. But the lawyer wanted to know what Jesus meant by "neighbor." Jesus' answer was the Parable of the Good Samaritan.

There was a wounded man lying on the side of the road going from Jerusalem to Jericho. A priest passed by and then a Levite. They walked past him without seeing if he was okay or offering assistance. Then a Samaritan man came along. Samaritans were social outcasts in that day. The Samaritan knew what it was like to be rejected by other people. In spite of the fact he had many reasons to be angry at the world, he was the only one who responded with compassion to the troubled traveler.

Note the two other people who first had an opportunity to help the wounded man were religious people, a Levite and a priest. Jesus posed the question, "Which of these acted as a neighbor?" The man's response was, "The one who showed mercy." 👬

Lawyer—Actually the man was not a lawyer in the contemporary 'judge and jury' sense of the word. In the New Testament, a lawyer was an expert in the details of the Jewish religion. He had excellent religious credentials. His life was spent studying the Law and teaching people to obey it. In putting Jesus to the test, he was likely seeking to catch a weakness in Jesus' teaching and lead the people back to the Pharisees.

© DIGITAL VISION

The road from Jerusalem to Jericho was a distance of around 17 miles. The road ran through rocky desert country, which provided places for robbers to surprise travelers.

A Good Samaritan?

Jesus' response to the lawyer was to tell him to love his neighbor. That is His command to us as well. We often have people in our lives with whom we would rather not associate, but Jesus commands us to *love* our neighbor, not ignore them.

Take a few moments to complete the categories chart below with the names of people who are in your circle of contact.

Family

Close Friends

Friends

Neighbors

Acquaintances

Enemies

Bear in mind that God calls us to love and minister to everyone you listed on the chart above.

History is full of examples of those who did not love their neighbors. Hitler's hate for the Jews in World War II resulted in the deaths of millions of Jews and the imprisonment of thousands of others. Many world leaders have attempted to wipe out entire races of people they did not like or who did not like them. Our own country's history is laced with prejudice and hate. Christ's command was (and is) to love. He showed the greatest example of love by laying down His own life for us. ▼

What About You?

Look again at the list of the situations you listed previously and the chart of people you identified. How should a Christian respond to these?

Is it possible that modern day believers respond to social outcasts in the same way they did in this passage?

If you were to begin ministering to one of these people, what would you do?

List below a strategy you might use to reach one of these groups? Remember, in this passage it was the outcast who reached out to one in need. How can you keep that in mind when reaching out to others?

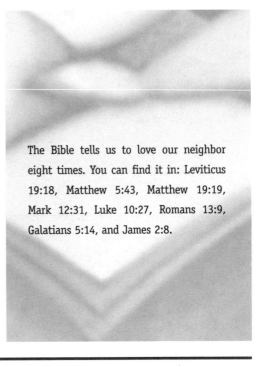

The Bible tells us to love our neighbor eight times. You can find it in: Leviticus 19:18, Matthew 5:43, Matthew 19:19, Mark 12:31, Luke 10:27, Romans 13:9, Galatians 5:14, and James 2:8.

 BEYOND THE BASICS!

- Memorize Luke 10:27.
- Choose one of the people you listed in "Identify Them" and make a decision to carry out your plan or strategy in reaching out to them.
- Write a modern day version of the *Good Samaritan* story that takes place on your school campus.
- Create a drama of the *Good Samaritan* story to be presented to your youth group. Make the setting modern or biblical.
- Survey those who live around you. Find out if there is a senior adult who might need some assistance around the house. Offer to help out.

---

1. Hullihan, Jim, "Broken Wing," *Chicken Soup for the Teenage Soul.* Deerfield Beach: Health Communications Inc. 1997.

19. Significant Worship

 Luke 19:28-40

MEMORY VERSE

God is spirit, and his worshipers must worship in spirit and in truth.

John 4:24

The Road to Stardom

Each season, thousands of young hopefuls try out for the reality TV program "American Idol." Many camp outside for days for their shot at stardom. American Idol judge Simon Cowell said, "American Idol is about being the best." Are they really the best? It comes down to opinion. Mark your opinions below.

1. What characteristic would you look for in an American Idol?
   ❑ Perfect voice ❑ Great look ❑ Great personality ❑ Good character

2. Why do people want to be an American Idol?
   ❑ Wealth ❑ Fame ❑ Success ❑ Purpose

3. Have you ever idolized a person because everyone else liked that person?
   ❑ Yes ❑ No ❑ I really don't want to say ❑ Maybe

4. What does the word "idol" mean to you?
   ❑ A symbol of an object of worship ❑ A false god
   ❑ An object of extreme devotion ❑ Pretender or imposter

You may be surprised to know all answers for #4 were taken from the *Webster's Collegiate Dictionary*. We normally think of an idol as a movie star, athlete, musician, or model everybody wants to be like. However, many times we have the wrong idea when we choose someone to be our idol. Sometimes we take it too far and that person becomes an object of extreme devotion, an object of worship—a "false god." In a sense, the title of "American Idol" can be accurate if the winner becomes the object of worship. He or she may be deserving of applause but not worship. When Jesus entered Jerusalem the week before His crucifixion, people may have seen Him as some ancient "Israelite Idol" but in reality He was and is the only One deserving of significant worship.

The King Is Coming...On a Donkey!

There are many ways to worship Jesus, but the greatest way to worship Him is to obey Him. Read Luke 19:28-40 and be creative when answering the following questions to learn more about genuine worship.

Name the different ways the two disciples with Jesus worshipped Him that day.

How did the whole crowd of people worship Jesus?

Why do you think the Pharisees told Jesus to rebuke or scold His disciples?

What do you think Jesus meant when He said, "I tell you that if these should keep silent, the stones would cry out"?

Based on everything you know about the following days of Jesus' life, do you think the people's worship was genuine?

Hosanna—Where Luke wrote the words "glory in the highest," the other Gospels record the words "hosanna in the highest." Hosanna was an expression of joy and praise for freedom that was either given or promised.

Prophecy—The Old Testament records a prophecy about Jesus riding on a colt hundreds of years before He actually did. Zechariah 9:9 says, "Rejoice greatly, O Daughter of Zion! Shout, Daughter of Jerusalem! See, your king comes to you, righteous and having salvation, gentle and riding on a donkey, on a colt, the foal of a donkey."

Worship—Worshipping someone or something means to esteem greatly, or think highly of that person or object. The person or object consumes our thoughts and decisions. Whom do you worship?

Jesus' disciples had no idea they were worshipping Him when they brought the donkey to Him, but they were! After being with Jesus for three years they knew to simply trust Him and obey.

As Jesus came into town on the donkey, the crowds laid their coats on the road and waved palm branches as a tribute to their King. They sang, "**Hosanna**" (Mark 11:9-10), and "Blessed is the King who comes in the name of the Lord! Peace in Heaven and glory in the highest!" (Luke 19:38).

Jesus knew He would be crucified at the end of the week. You might think He would slip into Jerusalem quietly. But He chose to enter town boldly and visibly, greeted by spontaneous expressions of worship.

Many in the crowd probably saw Jesus as a political Savior and did not understand His purpose. Some likely joined in because they were caught up in the excitement. However, there were those in the crowd that had seen Him heal. They had listened to Him talk. They knew He was different. These truly worshipped. Their expression to Him was very appropriate. ▼

Do you ever get caught up in the excitement of worship, without really understanding who you are worshipping? Does your worship fade into the background when someone new walks in? Write a prayer of confession in the space below. Ask His forgiveness for not recognizing who He is at times and for not worshipping Him with your actions on a daily basis.

Genuine Worship

Complete the following statements with a word related to worship. (*Answers can be found at the end of this session.*) Under each statement, write a sentence describing how the word relates to worship.

communication with God _____

use your voice to make a melody _____

false god _____

a way of life _____

quiet time _____

things you do _____

real or authentic _____

the reason you do something _____

BEYOND THE BASICS!

- Memorize John 4:24.
- Make an effort to worship God by having a personal quiet time or devotion everyday this week. Find a quiet, private place where you can really focus on God. Let go of your pride or embarrassment and worship God in whatever method you are comfortable.
- Write a worship letter to God during your devotion time. Don't ask for personal favors. Just praise God for who He is and thank Him for the things He has done for you.
- Make a list of ways you can worship God in your everyday life. Have you ever thought about being obedient to your parents as an act of worship to God? Have you ever thought about saying no to your friends when they ask you to do something wrong as an act of worship? Put into practice at least one of those ways each day.

Answers to page 120:
Pray, Sing, Idol, Lifestyle, Devotion, Actions, Genuine, Motive

Rate Your Worship

How do you measure up in the area of worship? Rate yourself on a scale from 1 to 7 (1 is never, 7 is always).

I focus on God and who He really is when I sing worship songs.

| 1 | 2 | 3 | 4 | 5 | 6 | 7 |

I forget everyone around me during worship time at my church.

| 1 | 2 | 3 | 4 | 5 | 6 | 7 |

I obey God's Word in my daily life.

| 1 | 2 | 3 | 4 | 5 | 6 | 7 |

God is most important in my life and there are no other idols that prevent my worship of Him.

| 1 | 2 | 3 | 4 | 5 | 6 | 7 |

I am faithful to worship God even when my friends turn away.

| 1 | 2 | 3 | 4 | 5 | 6 | 7 |

Total Score _____

10 or below = Need work!
11-15 = Better—But still need work!
16-25 = Average—Don't be mediocre!
26-30 = Above average—Good work!
31-35 = Excellent Job—Stay focused!

Think: What would it take for you to worship God as a lifestyle?

True Worship

by Andy Blanks

• The lights above the stage spin and shine, alternating colors to the beat of the music. Bright images flash across huge video screens as dancers speed through choreographed moves. The pop star dances from one end of the stage to the other, singing the lyrics to her newest hit single. Tens of thousands of fans in the audience hang on every word, sing every lyric, and scream the artist's name. The people on the front row stretch and reach at the chance to touch her hand.

• An hour and a half after the game is over, the crowd of people outside the arena wait by the door to the locker room. As the star basketball player finally emerges, the people crowd around him, congratulating him, trying to get his autograph, and calling his name as he makes his way to a luxury sports car. The fans press against his window as the car drives away, trying to get one last glimpse of the athlete.

• The teenage boy finally gets to sleep around midnight, after talking on the phone with his girlfriend for two hours. As he gets ready for school the next morning he looks at the picture of her hanging on his bathroom mirror. He arrives at school and immediately heads for her locker to walk her to her first class. Throughout the day, they spend all their free time together. That evening, like many evenings before, they will meet to watch a movie, to eat dinner, or to go to the mall. Before they go to bed they will talk on the phone for another hour.

Worship takes on many forms. We worship celebrities. We worship athletes and movie stars. We worship cars and cash, food and fashion. We worship people who don't deserve our worship. How do we worship these things? We worship celebrities, pop stars, and athletes when we improperly idolize them, when we honor them based on their ability to sing, dance, run, act, or simply look good in public. We worship money, food, fashion, and material things by allowing these elements to have an unhealthy place of importance in our lives. Basically, we waste a lot of time and emotion valuing things that have no eternal value. This is a harmful practice of which most of us are partly guilty. But it becomes an even greater problem when we are guilty of misdirected or improper worship of God. What is true worship? Let's look at what the Scripture has to say about how we should worship God.

True Worship is Obedience

As a Christian teenager living in what is mostly a non-Christian world, one of the most important ways you can worship Christ is by obeying Him. And you cannot obey Jesus unless you truly recognize who He is. The words of John the Baptist demon-strate this recognition: "The next day John saw Jesus coming toward him and said, "Look, the Lamb of God, who takes away the sin of the world. . . I have seen and I testify that this is the Son of God" (John 1:29,34). You cannot truly worship Jesus until you are ready to obey Him. You cannot obey Him until you recognize He is the Son of God. When you recognize this, you are ready to worship Him through your obedience.

True Worship is Giving God Your Best

Real worship involves giving God your life as an offering. Romans 12:1 says, "So here's what I want you to do, God helping you: Take your everyday, ordinary life—your sleeping, eating, going-to-work, and walking-around life—and place it before God as an offering. Embracing what God does for you is the best thing you can do for him" (MSG). By placing your life before God as an offering, you are saying to God you trust His ability to provide for you, and you are making yourself available for Him to use. This is your "spiritual act of worship." By worshipping God in this way, you open yourself up for God to reveal all the wonderful ways you can serve Him.

True Worship is Joy

Do you ever wonder why it feels so good to sing praise songs to God, why you feel so near to Him when you are singing music written just for Him? That is how He designed us! God "wired" us to worship Him through music. Psalm 81 says, "Sing for joy to God our strength...Begin the music, strike the tambourine, play the melodious harp and lyre." When His joy fills your heart, you overflow with praise to Him. God delights to hear your songs of praise, whether you are at church, in your car, or alone in your room. During your next quiet time, try singing your favorite praise song to God. Don't worry how you sound! To the Lord, the sound of your sincere worship is the sweetest sound of all.

True Worship is Humility

You can be obedient to God; you can offer your life to Him; you can praise Him with song. But unless you enter into worship with a spirit of reverence and humility, you are not giving God the honor He is due. Moses led an amazing life. God revealed Himself to Moses in so many wonderful ways—even in person on Mt. Sinai! In the story of the burning bush, God spoke to Moses through the fiery flames. But before Moses came any nearer to the bush, the Lord said "Do not come any closer . . .Take off your sandals, for the place where you are standing is holy ground" (Ex. 3:5). In biblical culture, taking off your sandals was a way of showing reverence and humility. In the same way, God demands a spirit of humility when we approach Him in worship and prayer. When you worship God, you are speaking with the Almighty Creator, the One who hung the stars in the sky and set the mountains in place. He knew you before you were born and knows every thought you will ever think. When you worship Him, realize Who it is you are worshipping, and humble yourself before Him.

All of Creation Worships God

God deserves and expects our worship and praise. The way in which we worship Him should reflect how we value Him. We need to be cautious of the value we place on worldly things. God is the only One worthy of our worship. He has done so much for us—blessed us with grace and mercy, eternal life, and forgiveness of sins. We should remember His blessings and worship Him accordingly. In the words of Psalm 150:6: "Let everything that has breath praise the Lord."

Modern Israel

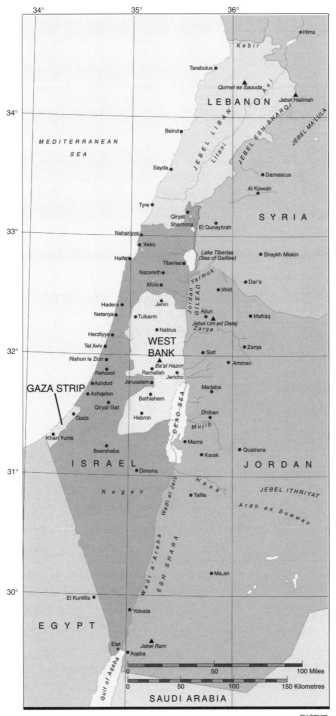

Compare the Difference—
Compare this map with the map on page 14. Borders have changed, and parts of ancient Israel are now within several other countries. Notice that Israel is surrounded by nations that are her worst enemies.

Map 4: Modern Israel

125

20

Born to Die

MEMORY VERSE

"This is my blood of the covenant, which is poured out for many for the forgiveness of sins."

Matthew 26:28

The Invitation

A close friend of our family received a special invitation to the White House for a dinner meeting with the President of the United States. My husband accompanied him to Washington, D.C. They flew together, stayed at the same hotel, ate their meals together, but when it came time to enter the White House for the meeting with the President, my husband stood outside the gate looking in. You see, his name was not on the invitation! He sat in a coffee shop, drank coffee, read the newspaper, and wondered what in the world was going on behind those gates. Actually, he never found out because it was a confidential meeting!

The Lord's Supper is by special invitation as well, and your name is written in big letters across the invitation's front! It is more special than being invited to the White House for a meeting with the President. It is a meal with the Lord Jesus Christ! Many times we think about the Lord's Supper as a time when we go through the motions of eating crackers and drinking juice as a ritual. But it is so much more than that. The Lord's Supper is an appetizer for the banquet we will enjoy with Christ in Heaven. It is a meal we eat together as Christians so we will not forget what the Lord Jesus Christ did for us on the cross.

Jesus' Last Supper

Jesus sent His disciples to prepare for the Passover Meal together. He chose the place, the time, and who would be there. He extended the invitation. Jesus was the host. He served the disciples. In John 13 Jesus actually washed His disciples' feet, including Judas (John 13:5-17)! The disciples were expecting the regular Passover meal they had eaten all of their lives, but Jesus gave new meaning to the Passover meal that night.

Read Matthew 26:26-30. Following each phrase below, fill in what this meal would represent from that night on. (*Answers can be found at the end of this session.*)

The Bread

The Cup

The Lord's Supper

Foot Washing—Foot washing was a form of hospitality extended to guests during Jesus' time. People walked from town to town on dry, dusty roads; therefore, washing their feet was hygienic and comforting. It was a job usually done by the lowliest servant in the house. In washing the disciples' feet, Jesus was modeling the kind of servanthood all Christians should imitate. See "Ya' Gotta Love" beginning on page 146.

A New Covenant—When Jesus said, "This is my blood of the covenant" (v. 28), He referred to the new covenant in Christ. The "old" covenant referred to the original covenant God made with Abraham, through which God promised to bless the Hebrew nation (Gen. 12:1-3). The old covenant was a covenant of laws sinful man could not perfectly keep. But the new covenant in Christ is one of grace and forgiveness.

The Lord Jesus Christ allowed His blood to be shed for many for the forgiveness of sins; therefore, we have a **new covenant** with God; not like the old covenant, where animal sacrifices had to be made again and again to cover our sins. It is a new covenant in which Jesus' sacrifice wipes away our sins. Jesus became the Lamb of God. ⊤ Whenever you have the opportunity to participate in the Lord's Supper, accept His invitation and worship Him with all your heart.

Your Last Supper

Jesus chose the bread and cup to symbolize His death on the cross. He gave us an object lesson we could experience to remember what He did for us. If you knew you would die tomorrow, what would you choose for your last supper? Could it symbolize something important you would want your family and friends to remember? Write out a menu for your last supper on the image at the left and describe what each item represents. For example, would you choose candy hearts for dessert to help your family remember how much you love them?

Jesus' Last Prayer

Matthew 26:30 says they sang a hymn and went to the Mount of Olives where Jesus prayed in the Garden of Gethsemane. Read Luke 22:40-46 and answer the following questions:

Twice in this passage, Jesus told the disciples to pray. What was His reason?

In verse 42, Jesus pleaded with the Father to "take this cup from me." Based on what you learned the cup meant during the Last Supper, what do you think Jesus meant by this?

When Jesus looked into that "cup of suffering," what do you think He envisioned?

My Prayer

Think about any unconfessed sin you may have in your life. It may be overwhelming at times to think about some of the things you have done in the past. Like Judas, maybe

Garden of Gethsemane—The Garden of Gethsemane (pronounced 'geth SIMM uh nee') is located east of Jerusalem and is just opposite the Temple. (See the map on page 151.) From its name, scholars think it was probably a lush garden situated in an olive grove. Matthew 26:42 offers one of the most touching scenes in Jesus' life, occurring at Gethsemane. This verse reveals a glimpse of the pain and uncertainty Jesus felt about His coming crucifixion. But as a model to all Christians, Christ submitted to the will of the Father, obedient even unto death.

BEYOND THE BASICS!

- Memorize Matthew 26:28.
- Read Exodus 12 to learn more about the history of the Passover.
- Read John 17 to learn what Jesus prayed in the Garden of Gethsemane. Make a special effort to pray everyday this week. Set aside a specific time. Pray like it is your last opportunity to pray on earth and see how it makes a difference in your life. You may want to write your prayers so you can look back and see how God answers your prayers.
- Think about a person you know who is not saved. Share with that person the meaning of Jesus' death on the cross this week.
- Get a plastic cup and decorate it with markers or stickers to represent Jesus' cup of suffering. Put it in a place where you will see it often to remind you of Jesus' love for you. Write prayers asking forgiveness for your sins and put them in the cup. You may choose to write in codes for privacy.

Answers to page 127:
The Bread—Jesus' body.
The Cup—Jesus' blood of the new covenant, which is poured out for many for the forgiveness of sins.
The Lord's Supper—Jesus' suffering and death on the cross.

you realize some things cannot be undone. But, that is why Christ died on the cross! He covered every last one of your sins! If you have not received Jesus' death on the cross for the payment of your sins, you can do that now. If you feel like there is no unconfessed sin in your life, then thank God for giving His only Son to accept your punishment. He loves you more than life itself! ⊤ Write a prayer to God telling Him what is in your heart today.

21

Examine Your Heart

 Matthew 26:47-56

MEMORY VERSE

So, if you think you are standing

firm, be careful that you don't fall!

1 Corinthians 10:12

The Greatest Commitment Ever

Months before Mel Gibson's movie, *The Passion of the Christ,* was released, people all over the world were in an uproar. He was accused of being anti-Semitic and greatly criticized for the violence in the movie. But, he made a commitment to make a movie that would show the world how Christ suffered for the sins of every person. He stuck to his commitment and even spent millions of his own money to make the movie. Now that is commitment—to put your money where you mouth is even in the midst of great criticism. It was kind of like Noah building the boat, or Abraham's willingness to sacrifice his son. However, that is not the greatest commitment ever made. The movie was about the greatest commitment ever made: Jesus' sacrifice to leave His glory in Heaven, to come to earth and be betrayed by His closest friends, to be beaten beyond recognition, to suffer the sins of every person from the beginning of time to the end of the age, and to die a cruel death on the cross. That truly was the greatest commitment ever made! ▼

Consider Your Commitments

In your life, you will make some commitments before you really understand the responsibility that comes with the commitment. Some commitments are short term, like a commitment to an athletic team or after school club; some are to be made for a lifetime, such as your commitment to your spouse. Greater still is the commitment you make to the Lord Jesus Christ. Fill in the blanks below as you consider commitments you will make during your life.

Present Commitments

Circumstances that cause a person not to follow through with commitment

Ways to follow through on this commitment

Future Commitments

Circumstances that cause a person not to follow through with commitment

Ways to follow through on this commitment

Betrayed with a Kiss

Read Matthew 26:47-56 and answer the following questions.

What did Judas do in this passage? What do you think caused Judas to break his commitment to Jesus?

What did the disciples do in this passage? What do you think caused the disciples not to keep their commitment to Jesus?

What could Judas and the other disciples have done to keep their commitment to Jesus? Consider the things you have learned in previous chapters. In the Garden of Gethsemane what did Jesus tell the disciples to do so they would not fall into temptation? How can this apply to your life?

Think about a kiss. What does a kiss mean? It is an action to show affection and love, but Judas chose a kiss to betray the One who loved him more than anyone. Why do

Judas Iscariot—Judas was one of the twelve disciples (and one of two named Judas; see Luke 6:16). He is always mentioned last in any listing of the disciples likely because of his betrayal of Jesus. His surname, Iscariot, means "man of Kerioth," which was a town in Judea located near the city of Hebron. Judas was in charge of the money pouch for the disciples, but John recorded that he was a thief (John 12:6). Judas struck a deal with the Jewish leaders to betray Jesus for 30 pieces of silver, which was equivalent to the wages a common laborer might earn in a four-month period. In his remorse over having betrayed an innocent man, Judas tried to return the money to the chief priests and elders, but they wouldn't take it. He threw down the bag of coins in the temple and then went away and hanged himself (Matt. 27:3-10). Acts 1:18-19 records what happened to the money and to Judas' body after his death.

The Kiss of Judas—Because two different Greek words were used for "kiss" in verses 48 and 49, there is an added element of treachery, even confusion, in Judas' kiss. In verse 48 when Judas said he would identify Jesus with a kiss, the Greek word for kiss is *phileso*, which was a typical greeting among friends. But in verse 49 when Judas actually kissed Jesus, the word used to describe the kiss, *kaephilesen*, means "to kiss fervently" and denotes love or affection. Some scholars believe even as Judas was in the throes of sin, the love Jesus compelled in him shone through in this kiss. Other scholars think Judas identified Jesus with a kiss as a way of pretending to come in peace so the other disciples wouldn't start a fight. Whatever the interpretation, the betrayal of Jesus by a man who had witnessed His entire ministry is heart wrenching and tragic.

you think Judas chose a kiss as the means of betraying Jesus? He could have pointed. He could have said, "This is Jesus." The Bible doesn't say specifically why Judas chose a kiss. Why do you think he chose this method to betray Jesus?

Betrayal Is an Inside Job!

In his book, *And the Angels Were Silent*, Max Lucado says, "Betrayal is a weapon found in the hands of one you love. Your enemy has no such tool, for only a friend can betray. Betrayal is an inside job." What do you think Max Lucado means by this quote?

© PHOTODISC

Think about a time you have been betrayed or abandoned by a friend. Write words below to describe how you felt. Circle the words Jesus must have felt when He was betrayed by Judas and abandoned by the disciples.

Think about Judas' commitment to Jesus. How was his commitment different than the other disciples' commitment? All of the disciples witnessed Jesus' miracles and power firsthand. Most of the disciples were truly committed to Jesus. They stuck by Him and tried to defend Him, but in the end they let fear overcome their commitment and scattered. Judas, on the other hand, witnessed these things as well, but for some reason he didn't get who Jesus was. He allowed his selfish desires to overrule his commitment to God's plan. He stole from the moneybag and intentionally sold Jesus out to His enemies. In the end, Judas realized he had made a terrible mistake, but the damage was already done.

Maybe there have been times you wanted to hit rewind on the video of your life and do it over again. Think about your commitment to Christ. Is it a true commitment, like the disciples, or are you just along for the ride? Maybe you have made a true commitment but have betrayed Jesus. Note that Jesus would have forgiven even the sins of Judas had he confessed and repented. Jesus is ready to forgive you as well! Simply ask Him. ▼

Write a prayer showing what is in your heart today:

 BEYOND THE BASICS!

- Memorize I Corinthians 10:12.
- Set aside a time to pray everyday this week. Find a quiet place where you will not be distracted. Prayer is an important way to avoid falling into temptation.
- Look out for troublesome times you may face this week. Stay close to God during those times and don't abandon your relationship with Jesus Christ.
- Ask God to show you a person who can be an accountability partner to you. Ask that person to hold you accountable for your quiet times and to pray with you this week. You may share difficult situations you are facing and ask this person to pray about those situations.
- Read I Corinthians 10:12-13. Write a poem or song expressing how God has helped you overcome temptation.

22.Jesus Loves Me, This I Know

 John 19:1-37

MEMORY VERSE

Greater love has no one than this, that he lay down his life for his friends.

John 15:13

Simple Faith

Karl Barth, arguably one of the most influential Protestant theologians of the twentieth century, was visiting Princeton Theological Seminary in 1961. By this time in his career he had completed the first 10 volumes of his *Church Dogmatics,* over 8,000 pages of theological writing. A *New York Times* reporter asked Barth if he could summarize his theology in a single statement. Barth responded, "Jesus loves me, this I know, for the Bible tells me so." It was as simple as that. This great mind could have answered with a lengthy and complicated theological run-on sentence. Instead he summed it up with a line from one of the most famous children's songs in the world. As simple as that phrase sounds, it really does capture the simplicity of the message of Jesus Christ.

Look up the words to "Jesus Love Me" in a Hymnal and jot them down below.

You probably know the first verse by heart. It captures the essence of the simplicity of devotion to Christ Paul talks about in 2 Corinthians 11:3. You can have a relationship with the God of the universe simply by trusting in the sacrifice of His Son to pay the penalty for your sins. Could it be any easier to understand?

Brutal and Bloody

After being betrayed by Judas, captured by the chief priests and Pharisees with the help of the Roman soldiers, and taken before the priests, Jesus stood before Pilate, the Roman authority figure in Jerusalem. Pilate tried to release Jesus because he found no fault in Him, but the people didn't want it that way, demanding the release of Barabbas instead (John 18).

Read John 19:1-3. The Bible does not spend much time describing what it was like for Jesus to be "scourged." This was a special form of torture reserved for slaves or those condemned to death for the worst kind of crimes. The victim was tied to a stake with his back exposed to the tormentors. The thongs of the whip were weighted with jagged pieces of bone or metal

"Jesus Loves Me"—The words of "Jesus Loves Me" first appeared in a book by Anna Warner in collaboration with her sister, Susan, published in 1860. In the novel, Johnny Fax, a young boy who is ill, asks his Sunday School teacher, John Linden, to sing a song. The teacher comforts the boy with the four stanzas of the hymn. William Bradbury wrote the tune, CHINA, for the words in 1861. The hymn was first published in 1862 in the *Golden Shower* Sunday School songbook. The song became very popular among Chinese children as a result of missionary work there.[1]

to make the blows more effective. The number of blows was left to the decision of the commanding officer. The victim usually fainted from the excruciating pain of the lacerations or even died from the severity of the wounds. Mel Gibson in his movie *The Passion of the Christ* provides the most graphic visual representation ever made of the scourging of Jesus. Watching his depiction is difficult due to the graphic nature of the violent act, but it gives a tremendous understanding for the suffering Jesus went through on our behalf.

Read John 19:4-37. Many people in the story thought they were in charge of what was happening to Jesus, but they were not. The Roman soldiers thought they were in charge; Pilate thought he was in charge; the Jewish religious leaders thought they were in charge; the people who demanded His crucifixion thought they were in charge. However, Jesus was in total control of His situation. Nothing happened to Him for which He was unprepared. He permitted all the events to occur. ▼ List specific instances where Jesus demonstrated control of His situation.

Bible Prophecy Always Comes True

God takes prophecy very seriously. Read Deuteronomy 18:18-22. The rules are pretty simple. If someone utters a prophecy and it doesn't happen, then the prophet is not speaking for God and should be put to death. Wow! One hundred percent accuracy required! Your life is on the line. You'd better make sure you heard God correctly. God doesn't take any chances when it comes to speaking to His people. He wants everyone to know precisely what He says.

Read John 19:1-37 again. List examples of Old Testament prophecies that were fulfilled in this part of the life of Jesus. There are three John specifically highlights, but there are others as well.

God wants to make sure you know everything you need to know in order to have a right relationship with Him. Part of that knowledge is the confidence that what He has said in His Word is absolutely true. We know Jesus was the Messiah prophesied to come long ago. We know He died in the manner told about hundreds of years earlier. We know that nothing is left to chance in God's sovereign plan. Jesus died when He died, right on schedule and according to His will and purpose. 📖

Finish It

Read John 19:30. What do you think Jesus meant by, "It is **finished!**"? What was finished? Jesus was willing to suffer the torture of a scourging and an excruciating (that word comes from the same root as crucifixion) death on a cross for you. You were worth that kind of sacrifice. He finished the work that needed to be done to pay the penalty for your sin. Hebrews 9:22 states, "Without the shedding of blood there is no forgiveness." Jesus had to die; there was no other way to satisfy the just requirement of God. ▼

Old Testament Prophecies of Jesus—One of the truly amazing things about the life of Jesus is the way in which Old Testament prophecies about Him were fulfilled throughout His lifetime. Josh McDowell states that there are over 300 specific prophecies in the Old Testament explicitly fulfilled in the life of Jesus. McDowell lists 61 of them in his book *The New Evidence that Demands a Verdict*.[2] A noted mathematician, Peter Stoner, found that the chance any man might have lived from Jesus' time to the present and fulfilled just eight of these prophecies is one in 10^{17} (10 to the 17th power). To illustrate, Stoner said if we take 10^{17} silver dollars and lay them on the face of Texas it would cover the state two feet deep. Then take one silver dollar, mark it, throw it back, and stir the entire mass. Next, blindfold a man and tell him he can travel anywhere in the state he wishes, but he can only pick up one silver dollar. What chance would there be that he would pick up the marked silver dollar on his first try? That chance would be one in 10^{17}. Stoner increases the prophecy number to 48. The probability is a staggering one in 10^{157} that one man could fulfill all 48 prophecies.[3]

BEYOND THE BASICS!

- Memorize John 15:13.
- Watch several crucifixion depictions from various movies, *The Jesus Film, Jesus of Nazareth, The Hope, The Greatest Story Ever Told, The Visual Bible* (all four Gospels), *The Passion of the Christ* (R rating for violence).
- Read Lee Strobel's *The Case for Christ* (Zondervan, 1998) or John Piper's *The Passion of Jesus Christ: Fifty Reasons Why He Came to Die* (Crossway, 2004).
- Read the section of Josh McDowell's book, *The New Evidence That Demands a Verdict*, pages 168-192 showing 61 Old Testament prophecies that came true in the life of Jesus.
- Identify a friend who does not know Jesus and initiate a conversation about the crucifixion of Christ. Use information you gained from the study to explain to your friend that Jesus died in our place.

It is Finished—The last words John said Jesus uttered from the cross was really one Greek word, *tetelestai*, which means, "It is finished." The other gospels don't record the words but say that Jesus died with a great shout upon His lips. So His coherent declaration was not a statement in weary defeat. It was a victorious proclamation of triumph. It was like someone exuberantly yelling "Touchdown!" when his team has completed a trek down the field. His work was done. He made the clear, conscious decision to give up His life once His task was complete.

Take a few minutes and write a prayer to thank God for what He did for you by sending Jesus to die on the cross in your place. Ask Him to help you live your life in such a way that it reflects your understanding and appreciation of His sacrifice for you.

1. *Handbook to the Baptist Hymnal*, Convention Press, 1992, p. 170.
2. Josh McDowell, *The New Evidence that Demands a Verdict* (Nashville: Thomas Nelson), pp. 168-192.
3. Peter Stoner, *Science Speaks*, (Chicago: Moody Press, 1963), p. 110.

23

Surprise Believers

 Luke 23:33-56

MEMORY VERSE

Yet to all who received him, to those who believed in his name, he gave the right to become children of God.

John 1:12

Deathbed Conversions

There are countless stories told of famous people who lived wicked lives and then decided to believe in Jesus Christ as their Savior at the last minute on their deathbeds. You may know of people close to your family who believed right before they died. The saying, "There are no atheists in foxholes," has been popularized by Christians claiming that when the chips are down people express faith in God to save them from imminent death. Do you believe that deathbed conversions are genuine? Make a list of people you have heard that have made last minute confessions of faith in Christ.

Paradise—This word appears only three times in the Bible: here, in 2 Corinthians 12:4, and in Revelation 2:7. It is used in each case as a reference to heaven. The exact location of Paradise is not the issue. Jesus was saying to this convicted criminal he would not have to wait for a future event but would have an immediate joyful experience with the Savior in heaven at his death. What an incredible promise to make to a man whose life was characterized by evil and who expressed faith only three hours before entering eternity.

References to the time of day in the Bible are sometimes difficult to understand. In verse 44 there are two—"the sixth hour" and "the ninth hour." The first century Jews started their daily clock at sunrise, roughly 6:00 a.m. So the sixth hour would be 12:00 noon, six hours after sunrise. The ninth hour would be 3:00 p.m., or nine hours after sunrise. Luke wrote this precise information for us to read because of what happened. Darkness covered the land for three hours, from 12:00 noon to 3:00 p.m. How incredibly unusual the sunlight would be hidden in the middle of the day. Yet it symbolically reflected what was happening on the cross; Jesus was bearing the burden for all the world's sin.

Just in the Nick of Time

Read Luke 23:33-43. The people watching the crucifixion hurled insults at Jesus. The religious rulers led by example as they sneered at Him. Jesus was hung on a cross between two thieves. One of them joined the crowd and insulted Him; the other asked Jesus to remember him in His future Kingdom, an expression of faith in who Jesus was. The unrepentant thief went to his grave and ultimately to hell. But Jesus promised to see the other thief that very day in **Paradise**.

Consider the implications of Jesus' statement to the thief. The man was a convicted criminal, probably a murderer because of the punishment he was enduring. Yet, he spoke words of belief in Jesus while dying on the cross next to Him. The thief didn't have an opportunity to perform any works in order to earn his salvation. He didn't have the chance to walk down an aisle or come to an altar in order to be saved. He didn't even have a chance to be baptized before his death. This is one of the strongest arguments for salvation by faith in Christ alone in all of Scripture. The thief was a surprise believer.

Centurion Belief

Read Luke 23:44-47. The centurion in charge of the crucifixion was a professional executioner. He knew his duties and responsibilities well. But what he experienced that day was different from other crucifixions. Rather than struggling to stay alive, this man chose the exact moment of His death. The centurion was not in charge; Jesus was in total control of the entire process. When the centurion saw what happened he "praised God." What an odd thing for an executioner to do. ▼

Read Matthew 27:45-54 and Mark 15:33-39. Complete the chart below based on the information you glean from each passage.

	Luke 23:46-47	Matthew 27:45-54	Mark 15:33-39
What time of day was it?			
What happened to the sun?			
What did they give Him to drink?			
What did Jesus say in His last moments of life?			
Who did they think He was calling to save Him?			
How was the veil torn?			
What other unusual things took place at His death?			
What did the centurion say after watching Jesus breathe His last?			

© PHOTODISC

Sanhedrin—Both Joseph of Arimathea and Nicodemus were members of the Sanhedrin. This was the highest Jewish tribunal during the Greek and Roman periods translated in the New Testament as "Council" in most English texts. The Council was composed of 70 members, plus the president, who was the high priest. In the time of Christ, the Council exercised not only civil jurisdiction according to Jewish law, but also some criminal as well. It was the final court of appeal for all questions connected with the Mosaic Law. It had the right of capital punishment until about 40 years before the destruction of Jerusalem. After that it could still pass, but not execute, a sentence of death without the confirmation of the Roman procurator. That is why the Lord had to be tried, not only before the Council, but also before Pilate. If this were not so, Jesus would have been put to death in some other way, probably stoning, for crucifixion was not a Jewish form of execution.

The Gospel writers were all inspired by God to write what He wanted them to write. When taken together we get a more complete picture of what happened. The centurion became a surprise believer, too.

V.I.P.s Are Convinced

Do you remember Nicodemus? He was the one that met secretly with Jesus in the night asking questions about salvation. (See "A Second Birthday" on page 106.) Well, he showed up again after Jesus was dead to help Joseph of Arimathea take care of His body. Read John 19:38-42. These two men were members of the **Sanhedrin**.

Answer the following questions:

What risks would these two men be taking in caring for the body of Jesus?

Why would they take those risks?

What sorts of risk are you taking in order to stand up for Jesus?

Are you willing to give up your social standing, your family relationships, and your plans for the future to be counted as a disciple of Christ? The Bible calls Joseph a "disciple of Jesus" (v. 38). He had made a choice to risk losing all he knew for the sake of knowing the Savior of the world. Nicodemus surely was a disciple, also; it is very unlikely he would have taken the same risk as Joseph had he not made the same choice. In fact, Nicodemus stood up for Jesus in a subtle way in John 7:50 and was sarcastically accused of being from Galilee. These two men became surprise believers, also.

Your Response

Are you trusting anything other than the death of Jesus on the cross to pay the penalty for your sins? Your good behavior will not impress God. Make a fresh commitment to trusting Christ. Express your total commitment to the sacrifice God made in the person of Jesus Christ on your behalf as completely sufficient for your salvation.

 BEYOND THE BASICS!

- Memorize John 1:12.
- Ask your Christian family members and friends if they have any relatives who decided to follow Jesus at the very end of their lives. Ask your family member if they believe the deathbed conversion was genuine or not.
- The Reformers of the 15th–17th centuries popularized the Latin phrase *sola fide*, which means "faith alone." Their point was that salvation was based on faith alone and nothing else. Go to www.graceonlinelibrary.org/theology/justification.asp to read some excellent articles and excerpts from eminent theological scholars on this important doctrine. ▼
- Ask God to put someone you know on your heart and mind you would never expect to believe in Jesus Christ as Savior, someone who would be a surprise believer if he or she ever believed. Begin to pray regularly for that person to trust in Jesus and for opportunities for you to be used by God in the process.

24

Ya' Gotta Believe

 John 20:1-18

MEMORY VERSE

For what I received I passed on to you as of first importance: that Christ died for our sins according to the Scriptures, that he was buried, that he was raised on the third day according to the Scriptures.

1 Corinthians 15:3-4

Surprised by Life

On August 19, 2003, Marilyn Manuel was declared a casualty along with 23 other UN employees after a suicide bomber's explosion shattered the UN headquarters in Baghdad. The family tearfully began preparing for her funeral. They started grieving the loss of their mother. She had officially been declared dead three days when the phone rang. Her younger son, Frederick, recalled picking up the phone in the early morning of August 21 and hearing his mother's strong clear voice saying she was alive and OK. Mrs. Manuel, who sustained minor injuries in the face, was mistaken for a Spanish military officer named "Manuel" who died in the bombing.[1]

Two thousand years ago, Jesus' followers were certain He had been killed only to be confronted later with a crisis of belief. Could Jesus have truly risen from the dead? Today we face the same crisis of belief. Do we believe in the resurrection of Christ? If so, how does that belief affect us? When His disciples heard His voice and saw Jesus alive, it changed the way they lived the rest of their lives.

Can You Believe It?

Note the ideas below many people believed in the past or still believe today:

- The world is flat.
- The sun and stars revolve around the earth.
- Tomatoes are poisonous.
- Man will never fly.
- Man will never walk on the moon.
- Touching a toad can cause warts.
- Jesus was never raised from the dead.

Some beliefs are relatively harmless while others can have serious consequences. In the following list, check those statements that include the greatest risk:

❑ If you sincerely believe strongly enough, you can jump off a building and fly.

❑ Breaking a mirror brings bad luck.

❑ Regardless of your religion, if you are sincere and good you will go to heaven.

❑ Forwarding certain emails to everyone on your list will bring you money, good luck, or a special blessing.

❑ It is not important that I believe Jesus was raised from the dead because a loving God would never let anyone spend eternity in a place as bad as hell.

Can you think of any belief worth risking eternity on? To put it another way: On what belief are you risking your eternal life?

Two Perspectives

Read John 20:1-8. Jesus had been hastily buried because the Sabbath was coming and Jewish law prohibited contact with a corpse on that day. Mary and several other ladies mentioned in the other Gospels went to the tomb early on Sunday to prepare the body for proper burial (Matt. 28:1; Mark 16:1; Luke 24:1). What they found was startling. Jesus' body was missing. Naturally, Mary ran to tell the disciples.

Sabbath—The Jewish day of worship is the Sabbath—the day of rest—which falls on Saturday. This is taken from the creation account in Genesis 2:2-3 and the Ten Commandments in Deuteronomy 5:12-14. Some Christian groups also worship on Saturday, but most worship on Sunday primarily because it is "The Lord's Day," when Christ rose from the dead. Colossians 2:16-17 reminds us that Christ, not the specific day, is the focus of worship.

Early—The Greek word for early in this case was *proi*, which was the technical word for the last of four divided watches during the night, sometime between 3 a.m. and 6 a.m. It was still dark when Mary and the others went to the tomb, indicating her deep desire to visit the body as soon as possible.

© PHOTODISC

"were lying there"—Strips of linen lying there—literally in the Greek: still in their folds. The phrase implies that the grave-clothes did not look as if they had been put off or taken off; they were lying in their regular folds as if the body of Jesus had simply evaporated out of them.

Peter and another disciple (likely John) raced to the tomb when they received word from Mary that Jesus' body was no longer there. Peter did not hesitate to enter the tomb first and assess what he found there. The linen wrappings "**were lying there**" and the piece of cloth that had covered Jesus' face had been rolled up separately. These were strong clues the body of Jesus had not been stolen. Why would a thief take the time to remove the wrappings and facial cloth from Jesus' body and then neatly place them back where they were? It is also unlikely robbers would have left the costly linens. As a result of the evidence John "**saw**" in the empty tomb, the Bible says he "**believed**."

Read John 20:9-18. Peter and John's reactions were practical while Mary's reaction was emotional. Still, it was Mary who was moved to action, and it was to her Jesus first revealed Himself after the resurrection. It is unclear why Mary did not initially recognize Jesus when He met her outside the tomb. Perhaps she was blinded by tears, or possibly the effects of the crucifixion had somehow altered Jesus' physical appearance. Certainly she did not expect to see Him alive. When Jesus called her by name, she knew who He was. Overwhelmed by joy, she grabbed hold of Him and called Him "Teacher." When Jesus directed her not to cling to Him, it probably had nothing to do with the state of His body. Likely His point was that she didn't need to hold onto Him as if He were going somewhere. His words indicated He had not yet permanently returned to His Father in heaven and so she should waste no time before telling the rest of His disciples He was alive. ▼

Your Response

Do you think Peter and John were convinced Jesus had risen from the dead? (v. 8) What evidence could have convinced them?

Why do you think Mary did not recognize Jesus?

Do you think you would have responded more like Peter and John or more like Mary? Why?

Saw—The Greek word for "saw" is *eido*. It means to see with belief. John did not understand all Jesus had foretold about His resurrection. The prophecy in Scripture did not convince him Jesus was alive. Nevertheless, love gave him eyes to read the signs in the empty tomb and believe Jesus had risen from the dead.

Believed—The Greek word *pisteu* means to respond in faith. In a sense John believed in what he had not seen. He had not yet seen the risen Christ. He had seen the empty tomb, and thus he believed Jesus had been raised from the dead. The same is true for us. We have not seen the physically resurrected Christ. We see the evidence of His resurrection and have an opportunity to believe.

BEYOND THE BASICS!

- Memorize 1 Corinthians 15:3-4.
- Call the closest non-Christian friend you have and set up a time to meet with that person for the purpose of sharing the story of Jesus' death, burial, and resurrection.
- Mary Magdalene said, "I have seen the Lord!" (v.18). Write a statement summarizing your own experience with the resurrected Christ ("I have been forgiven," "Jesus is alive," "He changed me inside out."). Carry it with you and say what you wrote to as many people as possible, recording the name of each person to whom you say it.
- Read and compare accounts of the resurrection and post-resurrection events in Matthew 28, Mark 16, and Luke 24 this week.
- Read the article on the evidence of the resurrection on the following pages. Read a book on the reality of the resurrection such as Josh McDowell's *The New Evidence that Demands a Verdict*.
- Visit a cemetery and read the tombstones. Write down the statements that have the biggest impact on you.

Headline News

On a separate sheet of paper, write a newspaper story covering the resurrection as if it had occurred in your town. Include quotes Mary might have said as the eyewitness.

What Do You Believe?

Check the statement you identify with the most:

- ❏ Knowledge of Jesus' death, burial, and resurrection are all anyone needs to respond to God.
- ❏ God works and speaks in distinct ways with each person to bring him or her to Himself.

Both are true. Jesus' death and resurrection made it possible for all people to come to God personally. ▼ The Holy Spirit works with individuals to convict them of sin and convince them of the need to follow Christ. ❱ Jesus reveals Himself to people in unique ways that draw them to Himself. ▼

---

1. Philippinenews.com, September 10, 2003, "Marilyn Manuel Comes Home."

Can You Believe What You Believe?

Andy Blanks

In 1985, the State of Maryland convicted and sentenced to death Kirk Bloodsworth for the murder of a young girl. Throughout the trial, Bloodsworth, a former Marine who had no history of wrongdoing, claimed he was innocent of the crime. But no one believed him. He spent nine years in prison before he convinced a court to look at a new technology that was being used to solve crimes: DNA testing. When the evidence from the crime scene was tested, it confirmed what Bloodsworth had been saying all along . . . he was innocent!

There is something about our human nature that makes it very difficult for us to believe something without seeing proof. Most of the time this is a good thing; it can keep us from believing outrageous claims about faulty products and fad diets, even from believing gossip about our friends at school. But is this kind of "seeing is believing" attitude healthy when it comes to our faith?

The Most Amazing Story Ever Told

Nearly two thousand years ago, people in Jerusalem were confronted with an amazing story, a story as miraculous as it was hard to believe. There was a man in their midst, an amazing man able to perform incredible miracles. He was making all kinds of bold statements. His name was Jesus, and among other things He said He was the Son of God, even God Himself! His most amazing claim was that He would be killed, but would come back to life three days later. This was truly a startling thing to say. Yet that is exactly what happened.

Jesus was indeed crucified, as He predicted. Three days after His death, Peter, John, and Mary, three of His most beloved companions, went to the tomb in which Jesus was buried. The course of history was forever changed by what they found: the tomb was empty. Jesus had risen from the dead, just as He said! How excited, scared, and amazed they must have been. All Jesus' words had come true; all His teachings were fulfilled. But was there enough evidence upon which to base their belief? Was there any real proof for their claim Jesus had risen from the dead?

Evidence for Belief

For thousands of years, Christians and non-Christians alike have argued over the evidence for Jesus' resurrection. This debate has resulted in numerous theories about the truthfulness of Christ's resurrection. Here are some of the more interesting arguments for positive proof of the resurrection of Christ.

The Empty Tomb

All four Gospels speak of an empty tomb. But where was Jesus' body? If the disciples stole it, as some people argue, they would have had to defeat the Roman guard that was assigned

to the tomb (Matt. 27:62-66). A Roman guard wasn't just one soldier, but a group of soldiers. These disciples were so scared they ran away when Jesus was arrested in the Garden of Gethsemane. Peter, one of the greatest disciples, denied three times he even knew who Jesus was! It doesn't seem logical these men could have defeated a group of Roman soldiers and stolen Jesus' body, and no one would have heard about it. If the Jews had stolen it, it seems like they would have been the first to admit it once Christianity started to spread so rapidly.

So we are left with Jesus' words: "We are going up to Jerusalem, and everything that is written by the prophets about the Son of Man will be fulfilled. He will be handed over to the Gentiles. They will mock him, insult him, spit on him, flog him and kill him. On the third day he will rise again" (Luke 18:31-33).

The Stone

All four Gospels mention that the stone placed in front of Jesus' tomb was rolled away. Most scholars agree this stone weighed between one and a half and two tons! Which argument makes more sense, that the disciples tiptoed past the Roman guard and rolled away this massive bolder without anyone noticing, or that it was the work of God?

The Disciples' Lives

Imagine for a moment you and several of your friends get together and decide to go around telling everyone your pet dog sprouted wings, flew into outer-space, and is now living on the moon. Of course, you and your friends know this is a lie, but you devote your life to telling everyone who will listen to you that it really happened. As a result, you are made fun of everywhere you go; people curse you, call you liars and troublemakers; some of your friends are put in jail; some of them are even brutally murdered for telling this story. Now, at some point in this process, if you and your friends are being abused for telling a story you know isn't true, don't you think you will admit it is a lie and, to keep from being mistreated, stop telling the story? Of course you would!

The disciples and other early Christians were in the exact same position. Because they went around telling people about Jesus' death and resurrection, they were imprisoned, tortured, and murdered. They were outcasts from society. Why would they go through all this trouble if they were making up the story of Jesus' resurrection? Wouldn't they just admit it was a hoax and go back to their normal lives? It had to be true or these men and women would not have sacrificed their lives for it.

Facts vs. Faith

The most amazing thing about the story of the resurrection is that it demands a decision from everyone who hears it. You have to decide whether or not you believe it. Why? Because Jesus said, "I am the resurrection and the life. He who believes in me will live, even though he dies; and whoever lives and believes in me will never die" (John 11:25-26). Belief in what Jesus said has eternal consequences. And while there is a wealth of evidence that points to the truth about the resurrection, at the most basic level, it is about faith. What will you believe?

• "Death Penalty Controversy." Oprah.com, *http://www.oprah.com/tows/pastshows/tows_2000/tows_past_20000928_b.jhtml. 29 January 2004.*
• Lang, Christopher Louis. "Historical Evidence for the Resurrection of Christ." Xenos Christian Fellowship, 7 March 1993, *http://www.xenos.org/classes/papers/doubt.htm. 26 January 2004.*
• McDowell, Josh. "Evidence for the Resurrection." Leadership U, 13 July 2002.
• *http://www.leaderu.com/everystudent/easter/articles/josh2.html. 26 January 2004.*

25

Better Than New

 John 21:15-21

MEMORY VERSE

*Humble yourselves before the
Lord, and he will lift you up.*

James 4:10

Bottom of the...

Have you ever experienced failure? Have you ever blown an opportunity to serve the Lord? In the space below, list different times you have "blown it."

Bad Decisions

I was invited to lead a group of ten freshman girls at a Disciple Now weekend. At the first break I began my one-on-one meetings with one of the girls. The host family set out the refreshments for the other girls but failed to notice three of them were gone. The first break ended and the doorbell rang. The youth minister walked in with the three missing girls. On his way to our house, he had spotted the girls rolling a house down the street. He stayed with them until they cleaned up the yard and then escorted them back to the host home. When they arrived, he made them apologize to our group for their actions. Needless to say the session that followed was a little tense.

Later that evening I was in my room preparing for bed when there was a knock on my door. My host dad said the youth minister was on the phone. The father had called him after finding the same three girls in his backyard smoking cigarettes. The youth minister wanted me to talk with the girls and decide whether they stayed or went home. These three girls had blown it. One of them was from a home where another Disciple Now group was meeting. The girls came into my room and we talked about the decisions they had made that night. We talked about the witness of their actions on themselves, our group, our host family and the church. We discussed how their actions were negatively influencing the weekend. Before we concluded our talk, one of the girls said, "I think we need to pray."

God is not a God of convenience. We can't turn our lives on and off with God, only calling upon Him in tough situations. Nevertheless, God *is* a God of grace and a God of the second and third chances.

Time Out
Talk with God about what you have written in the space on the previous page, about the times you have blown it.

A Man Called Peter
Who was this man Jesus loved, who was part of His inner circle, and who rose to the forefront as a leader among the disciples? Read the following Scriptures and write characteristics revealed about Peter in each passage.

- **Luke 5:1-7**
- **John 13:6-11**
- **Luke 22:8**
- **Acts 2:14-40**

- **Matthew 16:13-19**
- **Matthew 14:25-31**
- **John 21:17**

Did you use words like impulsive, Rock, undependable, stable, ambitious, boastful, humble, fisher of men, caretaker of the flock, one who denied, and proclaimer? Peter was all these and much more. From the first encounter Jesus had with Peter, He saw potential. He spent three years training him to carry out His mission. Yet, some of the characteristics that defined this man caused him to blow it at times.

Strike Three

Read Matthew 26:69-75. Peter fulfilled Jesus' prediction. He denied he knew Jesus. Peter was so overwhelmed with sorrow and shame by his denial that he may have felt he had struck out. The good news for Peter and for you is that Christ will not let you go! Read Mark 16:6-7. Peter may have chosen to take himself out of the game for a while but he was never off the team. 🏃

Team Meeting

Peter and the other disciples returned to what was familiar. They were fishing when Jesus appeared to them for a third time after His resurrection. He wanted Peter back in the game. He had a starting position for him. Read John 21:15-19.

Setting the Stage

During the Passover, Jesus told the disciples He would be betrayed (Matt. 26:31ff). Peter boldly stated that he would never fall away and would go with Jesus wherever He went. Jesus then informed Peter that not only would Peter run away, but he would deny Him has well. In the encounter in the Garden of Gethsemane, Peter indeed ran away from Jesus (Matt. 26:36-56). But even though Peter fled, he followed Jesus at a distance as He was led away to Caiaphas (Matt. 26:57ff).

© DIGITAL VISION

Lover—John used two different Greek words for love. However, they probably have the same meaning in this passage. Both *agape* and *philos* are used in John to describe the love between the Father and Son. Jesus was simply stressing the importance of Peter's love for Him.

Feed—Jesus used two different words for "feed." The Greek word used in verses 15 and 17 for "feed" carried a meaning of a shepherd that provided for his sheep. It was the word *boske*.

The word used in verse 16 was "take care of my sheep." It is the word *poimane*. The meaning of this word in Greek implied the care and guidance the sheep needed. If Peter really and truly loved Jesus, then his actions would reflect his love.

Peter was asked three times, possibly while he and Jesus were walking together (see vs. 20), if he **loved** the Lord. Notice the parallel with the denials. Peter denied Jesus three times, and in this passage he was asked if he loved Jesus three times. Likely Jesus wanted to be clear that He knew exactly what Peter had done. He also wanted Peter to be confronted with His grace.

How would you answer Jesus' question if He asked you, "Do you love me?"

Is your life daily reflecting your answer?

Game Plan

1st base: Feed my lambs

2nd base: Take care of my sheep

3rd base: Feed my sheep

Home Plate: Follow Me

(Answers can be found at the end of this session.)

Game Plan

Look again at John 21:15-19. Below each base to the left, describe what you think Jesus was commissioning Peter to do based on how He responded to Peter. Hint: your responses should reflect what loving God and loving God's people looks like.

Jesus commanded Peter three times to "*feed* my sheep/lambs." Jesus told Peter the kind of death he would have, one of crucifixion. Peter could have run away again but he stayed and accepted Jesus' commission. Jesus then challenged him after the prophecy of death with the words, "**Follow me!**"

Jesus' commission to Peter to feed His sheep was Peter's restoration. Jesus loved Peter so much that, in spite of Peter's denial, He commissioned him to take care of the people of God. Peter's restoration only occurred when he confessed true love for Jesus.

Jesus' call has not changed. Today, He is still calling people to follow Him. Following Jesus is a lifelong walk of faith. ⅄

Your Response

Spend some time writing a prayer to God asking the Holy Spirit to help you understand His grace. Ask Him to help you accept the forgiveness and restoration that come with a relationship with Christ. Before you get too task-oriented, be still and meditate on fact that God wants to use you.

Follow me—The Greek word Jesus used in this command was *aklougei*, which implies that Peter was to follow Him and keep following Him. Jesus didn't ask for a day of surrender, He asked for a life of daily surrender.

 BEYOND THE BASICS!

- Memorize James 4:10.
- Identify five people in your life whom Jesus has called you to "feed" and "take care of."
- Enlist an accountability partner of your same gender and ask him or her to help you be accountable in areas of your life where you can easily blow it (i.e. language, what you watch or read, or relationships).
- Discover through prayer what God is commissioning you to do and get busy doing it.

Game Plan, p. 158, your responses should be similar to these:
First Base—Jesus wanted Peter to guide His followers and provide for them;
Second Base—Jesus wanted Peter to minister to His followers;
Third Base—Jesus wanted Peter to love His followers as He Himself loves;
Home Plate—Jesus referred to the first command He had given Peter, Follow Me. The command had not changed. Jesus was saying, "Love and serve Me with all you are."

26. Discovering God's Agenda

Acts 1:4-11

MEMORY VERSE

But you will receive power when the Holy Spirit comes on you; and you will be my witnesses in Jerusalem, and in all Judea and Samaria, and to the ends of the earth.

Acts 1:8

Strongman Syndrome

In ancient Greek mythology, Hercules was the son of Zeus. His jealous stepmother, Hera, tried to murder him by putting a serpent in his cradle. As the myth states, young Hercules was born with great strength and killed the serpent. Eventually, his jealous stepmother drove Hercules insane. In his insanity Hercules killed his wife and three children and exiled himself in shame.

Hercules decided to ask the Delphic Oracle what he should do to regain his honor. The Oracle told him to go to Eurystheus, king of Mycenae, and serve him for twelve years. King Eurystheus couldn't think of any tasks that might prove difficult for the mighty son of Zeus, so Hera came down from her palace on Olympus to assist him. Together, the twosome came up with twelve tasks for Hera's mortal stepson to complete.

In many Greek mythological stories, the heroes ascended to heaven, usually by dying and becoming gods. In the same way after his death, the Greek god Hercules ascended to Olympus after completing his twelve tasks.[1]

Even today, we associate the myth of Hercules with a person being strong. Doing things within our own power is considered admirable. To the Greeks, Hercules worked his way into Olympus—a place of being in direct relationship with Zeus—through his own strength as if it depended on him. We would be in big trouble if having a direct relationship with God and entering the Kingdom of Heaven depended on us. Fortunately, God has graced us with His Holy Spirit to provide direct access to God.

In fact, Jesus ascended into heaven and promised to leave the Holy Spirit here in order to give us His power. Unfortunately, many of today's Christian students take on the Hercules approach: we think it is up to us to accomplish our "twelve tasks" in order to find favor with God.

Don't Just Do Something—Sit There

In Acts 1:4-11, the disciples were given a strong message "not to depart Jerusalem, but to *wait* for the Promise of the Father." But earlier didn't Jesus tell them to *go*? So which is it? Do they wait or do they go? Have you ever been faced with the "should-I-or-shouldn't-I" dilemma?

The disciples were eager for Christ to restore the kingdom of Israel, especially now that He was resurrected. Remember, the Jews had waited for generations to see the Messiah restore Israel. Jesus the Messiah had come. Now all that was left was for God to be united forever with His children! They were as excited as kids on Christmas—and then told to wait.

Describe a time you had to wait for something exciting (a trip, a birthday).

List three feelings you experienced as you waited:

What is one lesson you learned from waiting patiently?

© IMAGE STATE

Don't Just Sit There—Do Something!

But if all we do is sit around and wait and wait and wait…then we miss the point. God desires to accomplish work through His children. He intends for us to be His hands and feet. Jesus' final instruction to the disciples was to wait until they receive the necessary **power** that would come through the Holy Spirit. Jesus' word was to remind them not to move out until the supernatural power came upon them. He promised to provide a Helper. The Father promised to send a Guide or Counselor to provide the direction, insight, and ability to remember all we need to accomplish God's purposes.)

God is preparing us to accomplish His mission. He calls us to "be His **witnesses**" locally, regionally, and globally. God's purposes are the responsibility of every believer. Our job is not to jump out on our own power, but to wait to be empowered by the Holy Spirit.

After Jesus gave this final challenge to His followers, He was taken up into Heaven right before their eyes. Can you imagine? Vanished! Gone! Adios!

Not waiting and getting ahead of God:
- Displays a lack of trust
- Flaunts disobedience

Waiting on God's timing:
- Develops faith
- Allows us to see the most impossible of circumstances work out

Power—The Greek word for power is *dunamis (doo'-nam-is)*. We get our word dynamite and dynamic from this same root. It means miraculous power.

Witness—The Greek word for witness is *martus (mar'-toos)*. Because of the persecution the early witnesses faced, the word martyr came to mean a person who sacrifices something of great value (especially life itself) for the sake of principle.

Look what happened next in verses 10 and 11. Here is how *The Message Bible* describes it: "Why do you just stand here looking up at an empty sky? This very Jesus who was taken up from among you to heaven will come as certainly—and mysteriously—as he left." At times, Christian students are guilty of "just standing there looking up at an empty sky." And God is nudging them as if to say, "don't just sit there—do something!"

So, What Am I to Do?

Attempt to identify ways you can be a missionary (witness) to the world.

1. Journal

Journal your thoughts about the last moments Jesus spent with His friends. Read Acts 1:9-10. Take time to meditate on the experience the disciples had with Jesus. While He was in their presence, He was taken up and hidden by the clouds. Look up at the sky. Consider what the disciples must have felt as Jesus ascended. Write your thoughts about that experience as if you were there.

2. Discover

Sadly enough most people have the idea that missions must make you miserable. Before you plan to do any kind of service, explore these questions:

What do I enjoy doing?

What things bring me the most happiness?

What things do I enjoy so much that even when I am tired I have fun?

What are you going to do for a job when you "grow up"?

3. Dream

When Jesus last met with His disciples, He asked them to go to Jerusalem, Judea, Samaria, and the ends of the world. If you had an open ticket, a credit card with no limits and an interpreter, where would you go? What would you do? How would you be a witness to the world?

Destination:

My work assignment:

My plan for being a witness:

God wants to use all kinds of people with different gifts and abilities to let the world know about Him. Since you have been filled with the Holy Spirit, don't wait! You can do it now. Now that you have taken a look at your own desires, brainstorm some ways you can take your abilities and use them to be a witness.

----
1. http://www.hellenism.net/eng/heracles.htm.
2. http://www.imb.org/core/fastfacts.asp.

 BEYOND THE BASICS!

- Memorize Acts 1:8.
- Organize a group for a prayer walk in your neighborhood or near your church. For information about prayer walking go to www.waymakers.org.
- Look for simple opportunities to sacrifice something of great value this week in order for the people in your school or community to better understand the principles of Christ. Be the hands and feet of Christ to someone.
- Plan a service project in your city or state for your next school holiday.
- Adopt an area of the world to pray for. Create a world map for yourself or your Bible study group that features the men and women who work with this people group.
- Go on a short-term mission trip to another part of the world.

27. Undivided Attention

 John 14:15-18,25-27; 15:26-27; 16:7-14

MEMORY VERSE

But the Counselor, the Holy Spirit, whom the Father will send in my name, will teach you all things and will remind you of everything I have said to you.

John 14:26

The Long Separation

"Who's in the picture?" asked Dan. Freelance writer Dan Koeppel fingered the old and yellowed photograph he had found in his father's study. A stern image in military uniform with a scar sliced into his face stared back from the picture frame.

"That's my Uncle David," his father told him. "He lives, or lived, in Belize." Dan listened as his father told him the strange story of his great uncle. David served in the Polish army when World War II broke out. When Poland fell to Germany, David escaped. Frustrated and angry, he joined the British Army where he served out the war. The family migrated to America after the war, but not David. Mostly forgotten by his family, he wandered from place to place finally landing in British Honduras, now called Belize. "I doubt if he is even alive any more," Dan's father told him. "He would have to be in his 80's."

The harsh face captured Dan's imagination. Could Uncle David still be alive? What had become of him? The picture of this lost uncle crept into his mind over and over again. Then, Dan landed a writing job that would take him to Belize. Immediately, he decided he would try to find his lost uncle.

When he arrived in Belize, Dan was surprised to find out his Uncle David had been a well-known doctor. Stories about him led Dan from one remote village to the next. Finally, he was directed to a crumbling home. Dan stood at the gate, hardly believing he might have found his long-lost great uncle. He rang the bell on the front gate, but got no response. "David?" Dan yelled out. "David Koeppel?"

"Who's dat?" a gravely voice yelled.

"I'm your brother Morris' grandson," Dan yelled back.

A curious, wrinkled face peered out. He was eighty-six years old and blind in one eye. He stared long at Dan. Finally, he spoke. His response brought a lump to Dan's throat. He said, "I thought I had been forgotten."[1]

In a few short years, Jesus had become closer than family to His disciples. They had witnessed His crucifixion, and had seen Him alive after His resurrection. They stood awe-struck as Jesus ascended out of sight into heaven. To be left alone to carry on Jesus' work would have been awful. But Jesus never intended to leave them on their own. Even before His death, Jesus promised His disciples the Holy Spirit would come to them.

Never Orphans

Try to imagine what it would be like to be alone in the world. Write a few words that come to mind for you here:

Read John 14:15-18. Did you catch what Jesus told His disciples? They would not be orphans. The **Holy Spirit** would always be with them.

27.Undivided Attention

Trinity—One of the hardest things for many people to understand about God is how He can be three persons (Father, Son, and Holy Spirit) and still be only one God. The Bible is very clear that God is one God. (See Deut. 6:4.) At the same time, the Bible describes the work of each person as being distinct. (See 1 Peter 1:2) If you have a hard time understanding the Trinity, you are in good company. The church has agreed that the Trinity is a mystery since its earliest days. GOD

The Holy Spirit—The Holy Spirit is the Third Person of the Trinity. To say the Holy Spirit lives within us is to say God lives within us. When Jesus told the disciples He would send the Holy Spirit to them after He had departed, it was not really another who would replace Jesus; it was the Spirit of Jesus Himself. The Holy Spirit reveals God's will to us. He empowers us.

The Spirit will always be with you in your life if you belong to Him. What does that mean to you?

❑ I never have to eat my Cheerios alone.
❑ Someone loves me even when I mess up.
❑ I can attempt great things because I'm not doing them alone.
❑ I am loved even if my Hawaiian shirt is out of style.
❑ My friends may abandon me; the Holy Spirit never will.
❑ When I am hurting, someone knows…and cares.

You may have checked all these and written some of your own thoughts as well. When you realize God's Spirit is always within you, it can change the way you live. Think about your life. Does it show evidence you are aware of the Holy Spirit within you? Mark your answer on the scale below. (One means you never have that awareness; 10 means you always have that awareness.)

1	2	3	4	5	6	7	8	9	10

Try saying the following prayer right now. Repeat it several times.

Holy Spirit,
help me to be constantly aware
of Your presence in my life.
Help me to experience Your love
for me whatever I may go through.

The Work of the Holy Spirit

Jesus taught His disciples about the work of the Holy Spirit in the days before His death, explaining to them that the Holy Spirit would always be present.

Jesus promised the Holy Spirit would be a Teacher. It would have been great if the disciples could have understood all of Jesus' teachings while He was on earth. Unfortunately, people don't learn God's truth like that. Read John 14:25-27. What two things did Jesus say the Holy Spirit would do as their Teacher in verse 26?

1. The Holy Spirit would
   _____ them _____ things.
2. The Holy Spirit would
   _____ them of _____
   Jesus had said to them.

Counselor—The Greek word Jesus used in John 14:16 is *paraclete*. A paraclete was someone who was "called in." For example, it might refer to a person who was called in to testify on behalf of someone in a court trial. It might refer to an expert called in to give advice. God is often referred to as a counselor. (Check Ps. 16:7; 32:8; 33:11 and 73:24.) The picture Jesus was painting for His disciples was that the Holy Spirit would be a constant source of help and encouragement for them. ❜

Conviction—The Greek word used in the passage for "will convict" is *elegsei*. Conviction is the work of the Holy Spirit. He causes people to realize their own sinfulness. He convinces people of the righteousness of Jesus Christ and causes us to realize how far we are from the righteousness of Jesus. He gives people awareness that they ultimately must face judgment. A person will only be convicted because of the work of the Holy Spirit.

- Memorize John 14:26.
- Begin a journal to reflect on the Holy Spirit's work in your life. Write down things you believe the Spirit is teaching you, times when He brings conviction in your life, and times when you sense a special nearness with Him.
- Copy Psalm 139:23-24 from your Bible. Read it as a prayer to God each day this week. Invite the Holy Spirit to speak to you about areas of your life you need to bring in line with His desire for you.
- Interview key leaders in your church or youth ministry. Ask them about how they experience the work of the Holy Spirit in their lives.
- Start a prayer journal for your Bible study group. Take responsibility for keeping it updated and spending personal time in prayer about the requests.

The same Holy Spirit who guided the disciples as they began the first church is living inside you.

Read John 15:26-27. The Holy Spirit speaks to believers about the truth of Jesus Christ. That isn't where it stops. The Spirit leads us to testify about Jesus.

Write the name of one person you know who needs to know the truth about Jesus.

The Holy Spirit would bring conviction. Read John 16:7-14. According to this passage, the Holy Spirit will **convict** the world of guilt in regard to what three things?

1. _____, because men do not believe in me;
2. _____, because I am going to the Father;
3. _____, because the prince of this world now stands condemned.

---

1. "A Very Good Place to Disappear," Dan Koeppel, *National Geographic Adventure*, April 2002, pp. 45-49.

28.Are You Ready?

 Matthew 24:3-14,30-31,36-44

MEMORY VERSE

Therefore keep watch, because you do not know on what day your Lord will come.

Matthew 24:42

Predicting the Second Coming

He claimed to be a new Elijah. He promised to begin the reign of God on earth. Victor Houteff was leader of an unusual cult called the Davidian Seventh-Day Adventist Association. He believed he would bring about the return of Christ. His followers expected to see God do amazing things. What a shock it was to his followers when Houteff died in 1955 without any of his prophecies coming to pass.

Houteff's wife, Florence, took over the leadership of the cult. Florence told her husband's followers Jesus would return on April 22, 1959, 1,260 days after her husband's death. She based this on a prophecy in Revelation 11:3. Followers of the sect began to gather at New Mount Carmel, a camp near Waco, TX, owned by the cult. They planned to await the return of Jesus there. Needless to say, Jesus didn't return. Florence admitted her errors and dissolved the Davidian Seventh-Day Adventist Association.

Florence sold Mount Carmel to the leader of a splinter group called the Branch Davidian. Later, their leader, David Koresh, began teaching that he was the "Lamb" from Revelation 5 who would bring about the second coming of Jesus Christ.

Over and over again, people have announced they know the time of Jesus' return. All of them have been wrong. What have you heard about Jesus' Second Coming? Make some notes here.

The Course of History

Where is history headed? Most people throughout history have believed history is moving toward a decided outcome. There is good reason to believe this because the Bible teaches that the world is rushing toward the return of Christus.

Read what Jesus said in Matthew 24:1-14, 30-31. This passage has some confusing statements, but focus on the picture of the future Jesus was painting for His disciples. As you read, list things Jesus told His disciples to expect in the space below.

It is difficult to understand all Jesus said. Don't get bogged down in trying to explain everything Jesus said would happen. Instead, concentrate on the main points Jesus made. *(Answers can be found at the end of this session.)*

1. The coming of the Son of Man will be like lightning;
   it will be _____ to everyone.

2. There will be _____ _____
   that will try to deceive people.

Jesus is coming back. When He does, everyone will know it. His coming will be clearly visible to everyone. Until that time, many things will happen.

False Prophet—A false prophet or teacher ignores the truth of Christ. Instead, he teaches his own opinion as truth. He attempts to draw people to himself rather than lead them to follow Christ. The test of a teacher is the extent that they point people to Christ.

The Return of Jesus—The Bible never uses the words "the second coming." The word used for the return of Christ is the word *parousia*. The word was used to describe the coming of a king to his subjects. It describes a coming with authority and power. The *parousia* of Christ is the one event towards which all creation is moving.

Some will claim to be the Messiah or will claim to have the truth of God. Many will be drawn to **false prophets** instead of accepting the truth of Jesus Christ. However, God's people will keep their focus on Christ until the end.

Headline News

The **return of Jesus** would definitely be headline news. If you were responsible for creating a headline for His return, what are some possible phrases you would use? The objective is to help people understand that they need to be prepared for His return. Write some phrases in the space below.

Jesus never deceived His disciples. Following Him would not mean an easy, trouble-free life. In fact, He promised His followers they would be hated, persecuted, and even killed (Matt. 24:9). Many will act like Christians for a while, but will give up when things are too hard. Those who have truly committed their lives to Christ, however, will remain loyal to Christ to the end.

Now or Later

Read Matthew 24:36-44. When will the coming of Christ be? How can we know when He will return?

What are you supposed to be doing to prepare for His return?

You probably picked up on the fact you can't know when Jesus will return. Jesus said no one knows except God. His plan for you is not to create a timeline to figure out when Jesus will be coming back. Rather, He wants you to be ready for His return at all times.

Make a list of things you did yesterday. What were the things that occupied your time from the time you got up until you went to bed again?

© DIGITAL VISION

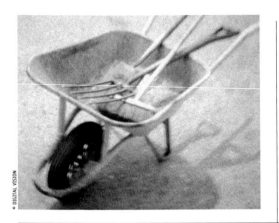

Now, suppose you knew Jesus was going to return tomorrow. With Jesus' return, everything would change. What would you do differently today if you knew Jesus would return tomorrow?

Do you get the point? God's intention is that you live everyday as if Jesus were coming back immediately. And He might.

Are You Ready?

Use the acrostic below to describe how you can be ready for the return of Christ. Write a sentence or word for each letter of the word "ready" to describe how you can personally be prepared.

R

E

A

D

Y

 BEYOND THE BASICS!

- Memorize Matthew 24:42.
- Call a friend you haven't talked to in a long time. Plan a time to get together and catch up on each other's lives.
- Send an encouragement card to someone who is not as strong in their faith as they once were.
- Take time to visit with an elderly person, like your grandparents or someone near their age. Ask them if they were ever concerned they were living in the last days when they were teens.
- Do video interviews with some of your friends. Ask them, "Are you concerned that Jesus will return during your lifetime?" Record their answers and share them with your Bible study group.

Answers to page 171:
1. visible
2. false prophets